LOVABLE
Beaded Creatures

LOVABLE
Beaded Creatures

Anja Freese

Sterling Publishing Co., Inc.

New York

Translated from the German by Daniel Shea

Library of Congress Cataloging-in-Publication Data
Freese, Anja.
Lovable beaded creatures / Anja Freese
     p. cm.
ISBN-13: 978-1-4027-2866-2
ISBN-10: 1-4027-2866-2
  1. Beadwork—Patterns. 2. Animals in art. I. Title.
TT860.F74 2006
745.58'2—dc22   2006040342

10 9 8 7 6 5 4 3 2 1

Published by Sterling Publishing Co., Inc.
387 Park Avenue South, New York, NY 10016
Originally published in Germany by Englisch Verlag GmBh, Wiesbaden
under the titles *Plastisch schöne Perlentiere* © 2001; *Neue Perlentiere:
Plastisch schön* © 2002; *Perlenfiguren: Fantastisch Plastisch* © 2003; and
Perlen: Figuren und Schmuck fädeln und weben © 2004

English Translation © 2006 by Sterling Publishing Co., Inc.

Distributed in Canada by Sterling Publishing
c/o Canadian Manda Group, 165 Dufferin Street
Toronto, Ontario, Canada M6K 3H6

Distributed in the United Kingdom by GMC Distribution Services,
Castle Place, 166 High Street, Lewes, East Sussex, England BN7 1XU

Distributed in Australia by Capricorn Link (Australia) Pty Ltd.
P.O. Box 704, Windsor, NSW 2756, Australia

Manufactured in China
All Rights Reserved

Sterling ISBN-13: 978-1-4027-2866-2
        ISBN-10: 1-4027-2866-2

For information about custom editions, special sales, premium and
corporate purchases, please contact Sterling Special Sales
Department at 800-805-5489 or specialsales@sterlingpub.com.

Contents

Introduction

For years, beaded animals and animal jewelry have brought enjoyment to young and old alike. Gaining inspiration from my childhood stuffed animals and clay figures, I continue to discover new beaded friends. As you read the following pages, allow yourself to be surprised by what can be done with beads: the Wise Owl will inspire you, and the Honey Bear will make you smile. All the projects included here are easy to make—the technique itself is not difficult at all. If you carefully follow the instructions on these pages, then nothing should come between you and your crafting fun.

I would like to express my gratitude to all those lovely people who tirelessly inspire me with new ideas. I wish you lots of joy with these fun and creative projects.

PART ONE

Beaded Animals

Getting Started

Materials

BEADS

Rocaille beads, also called e beads or Indian seed beads, can be purchased in various colors and sizes in craft stores and over the Internet. You can choose among matte, glossy, iridescent, or metallic-colored beads with various linings. When crafting the beaded figures in this book, we used size 8 (also referred to as size 8/0 in some outlets) Rocaille beads with a diameter of 2.5 mm, about 10 beads to an inch. In a few projects, size 7 (7/0) and size 6 (6/0) black beads with diameters of 2.6 to 4 mm are required for the snout or nose of an animal.

TIPS: Bead width can vary tremendously depending on the manufacturer and the individual type of bead (glossy, metallic, etc.); therefore, pay close attention when you purchase your beads: be sure to select beads of equal size. If the beads you use vary too much in size, the body of your project may be out of proportion.

Color names vary widely. It is best to match the color, finish, and lining you see rather than order by color name.

BRASS WIRE

You will need brass wire with a diameter of 0.3 mm in order to string the beads. For the most part, you can allow a wire length of about 65 in (170 cm) for the bodies of the figures, though some require significantly more. Read the materials lists carefully to ensure that you have enough wire for the project you're planning. Excess or protruding wire can always be cut off and reused for smaller details, such as ears. For larger body parts, such as legs, choose a wire length of about 31 in (80 cm); for smaller details, use a wire length of 12 to 20 in (30 to 50 cm).

TOOLS

You will need a pair of scissors for clipping the wire and a pair of flat tweezers to pull the wire through the beads and to twist the wire ends together.

Techniques

BASIC TECHNIQUES

1. Thread the first row of beads onto the center of the wire.

2. Using one end of the wire (thread A in this illustration), thread the second row of beads.

3. Take the opposite end of the wire from step 2 (thread B in this illustration) and thread it through the second row of beads in the direction opposite the one you used for thread A.

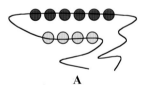

A

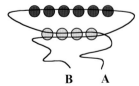

B   A

4. Firmly pull on both ends of the wire to tighten the beads. Follow these steps for all consecutive rows in the basic technique.

TIP: As you work, do not allow the wire to form loops— the wire may break as you tighten it.

5. To make the animals' bodies three-dimensional and to make them appear lifelike, you will alternately bend rows up (a top row) and down (a bottom row) in a rounded manner. In this book, when you see two rows drawn between two lines, you are to bend the first row up and the second row down. The numbers beside the rows indicate the number of beads for each row.

5	●●●●●	top
5	○○○○○	bottom
5	●●●●●	top
5	○○○○○	bottom

Rows not divided by lines remain flat instead of being bent up or down. At the intersection of the top and bottom rows, you will see that the wire looks like a zigzag line. This zigzag line must be kept as small as possible by pulling the wire tightly as you thread the beads.

SEAHORSE TECHNIQUE

Some animals require a modification of the basic technique, since parts of their bodies have a strong bend to them, for example, the tail of a seahorse (see page 46). A downward bend is made by leaving out a bottom row, which means that two consecutive rows are bent up after one row is bent down. Rather than threading beads on the "missing" row, draw the wire through the existing "belly row" (a row on the underside, or belly, of the figure) a second time. With an upward bend, a "back row" (a row on the top, or back, of the figure) is left out. In the instructions for this technique, you will find three rows drawn between two lines. The rows that have to be bent up or down are noted to the right of the illustration. In addition, the numbers listed to the right indicate the order in which the wire should be pulled through the individual rows of beads.

3	●●●	top 1
2	○○	bottom 2 4
3	●●●	top 3
3	●●●	top 5
2	○○	bottom 6 8
2	○○	top 7

Both wire ends will be pulled twice through the rows that are noted with two numbers. The following illustration demonstrates how the wire is threaded through the beads. For clarification, one wire end is colored gray and the other black.

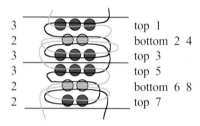

In a similar manner, the upward bend is worked as illustrated below.

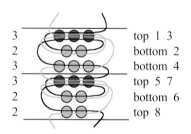

TIP: It is much easier to pull the wire through a row of beads several times if the wire ends are smooth and straight. So, if you need to, cut off a short piece at the end of the wire to make it smooth and straight. Also, do not be afraid to straighten out rows of beads as you are threading your wires, since you can easily manipulate the beaded figures back into their correct shapes.

ORDER OF ROWS

Bead the bodies of the animals first, starting with the head. (For jewelry, follow the instructions given for each piece.) The rows are strung one after the other from top to bottom, and the animals' arms, legs, fins, and so on are attached to the completed body.

EARS, LEGS, AND FINS

With a few exceptions, separate pieces of wire are used for various details of some animal bodies, such as ears, legs, and fins. Each project's instructions indicate where the necessary wire should be pulled in. It's often easier, however, to thread the additional wire into the body before tightening that particular row of beads.

VARIATIONS

Variant 1. This variant is used to attach the legs to the right and left sides of the body. A piece of wire for each leg is pulled through the beads positioned in the middle of two belly rows. The right leg is formed with the two wire ends pulled through the right side and the left leg with the two wire ends pulled through the left side.

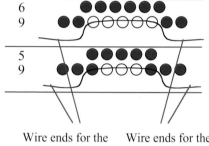

Wire ends for the left leg   Wire ends for the right leg

Variant 2. Occasionally, the ends of only a single piece of wire are required, which is the case for ears, for example. In this variant, two pieces of wire are pulled through the marked beads of the upper row. The left ear is created with the ends of the left wire and the right ear with the ends of the right wire.

Wire ends for the left ear   Wire ends for the right ear

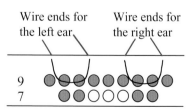

Variant 3. For some fins, the wire is simply pulled diagonally across the back or the belly of the body. In this example, the wire is pulled under the three rows of the back.

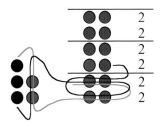

In relation to the body, the technique looks like this:

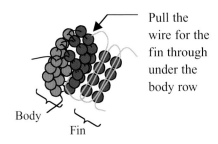

Pull the wire for the fin through under the body row

Body
Fin

Variant 4. For other fins, the rows of beads do not run diagonally across but parallel to the rows of the body. In this variation, a wire loop is pulled through under a body row, for each of the fin rows.

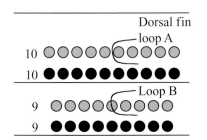

Dorsal fin
loop A
10
10
Loop B
9
9

In relation to the body, the technique looks like this:

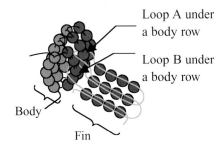

Loop A under a body row

Loop B under a body row

Body
Fin

Variant 5. In some cases, no extra piece of wire is needed for crafting small details, such as ears or thin legs. The instructions will clearly state when this is the case. In addition, specific instructions are provided regarding the required wire lead, as shown in the illustration here, and as is the case with the ears in the Shrew, project 10, for example.

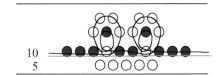

10
5

EYES

To allow your beaded animals to look more vividly into the world, you should choose large (wide) beads for the sparkling black eyes; you may want to use size 7/0 (3 mm) beads instead of the usual size 8/0 (2.5 mm) Rocaille beads.

STABILIZING YOUR FIGURES

It is always important to tighten the wire well as you work so that your creations maintain their shape. In some projects, such as the Fawn, I recommend that you provide additional support to the body. This is easily done: when your figure is completed, simply pull the protruding wire ends (or a new piece of wire) through the figure, in between the wires that are visible on the sides, as one does with embroidery. Pull the wire ends tightly to stabilize the figure.

THREADING THE WIRE ENDS

You can choose from several possibilities to thread in the wire ends when you finish beading or need to begin a new section.

1. Thread the wire ends through one or two previous rows.

2. Thread one wire end through a nearby row to the other wire end and twist the two ends together.

3. Wrap both wire ends several times separately around the leading wire.

Duckling

Ducks are also called waterfowl because they are normally found in places with water, like ponds, streams, and rivers. Ducks have shorter necks and wings and a stout body compared to their swan and goose cousins. Ducks have webbed feet that act like paddles and allow them to swim with ease. In fact, ducks waddle instead of walk because of their webbed feet. Ducks were wild until they were domesticated by the Chinese hundreds of years ago. There are many different species of wild duck. Most of the farm ducks are a species called Pekin, which have white or cream-colored feathers and orange-colored bills. They do not fly and do well in captivity. The Pekin duck is the most popular breed in the United States.

Instructions

Prepare the beginning of the beak in the ninth body row by threading two beads by means of a deviating wire that serves as a hanger for the beak (see illustration). As you shape the beak, review the

MATERIALS

- Rocaille beads in pale yellow, orange, and white, size 8/0 (2.5 mm)
- 2 Rocaille beads in black, size 7/0 (3 mm)
- Wire: 70 in (170 cm) for the body; 3 x 12 in (30 cm) for the feet and tail; 2 x 15 in (40 cm) for the wings; 25 in (60 cm) for the beak

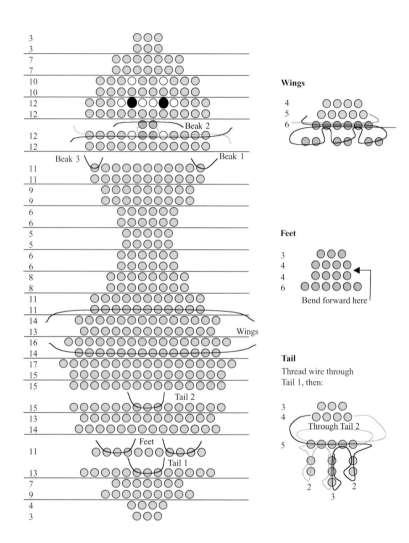

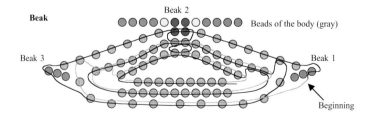

crafting instructions and illustration carefully, since this threading technique deviates widely from the basic technique. First, draw a wire through the section marked "Beak 1" (variant 2). In the two upper rows of the beak, create hangers for each of the subsequent rows. Attach the wings to the body by means of variant 1. You can affix the feet and tail to the body using variant 2. The wings remain completely flat, but bend the feet upward at the second row; the rest of the feet remains flat. When crafting the tail, pull a wire through the section marked "Tail 1." After the third tail row, pull one wire end through the beads of the body marked "Tail 2" and then right back through the third tail row. Finally, shape the tail feathers by means of the special wire lead. To stabilize the neck of the Duckling, thread a wire through the wires that are visible on the side, as is done in embroidery. To allow the duck to sit, press the two last body rows slightly inward.

Rooster

All domestic fowl are descendants of a single wild species: the Bankiva chicken. As early as 2500 BCE, Bankiva chickens were kept as pets in India; a thousand years later, these domestic fowl were also widely spread in China and Egypt, where large amounts of eggs were incubated simultaneously in artificial incubation facilities. In Europe, domestic fowl were kept several hundred years BCE for their eggs and meat. Birds were not domesticated in the Americas until the arrival of the Europeans. With a marvelous variety of more than 150 breeds, these animals are still valued for their meat and egg production.

Instructions

Push the last four body rows slightly inward so that the rooster can sit. After each row of beads, you will repeatedly affix the comb to the head. First, pull the wire through the point marked "Comb 1" (variant 2), and string the first row; then pull the two wire ends in opposite directions through the beads of the point marked "Comb 2," and string the beads of the second row; and so on. Press the comb together firmly on each side. Attach the beak, the flaps of skin (or wattle), and the feet to the body using variant 2; attach the wings to the body by means of variant 1. With the exception of the beak, these body

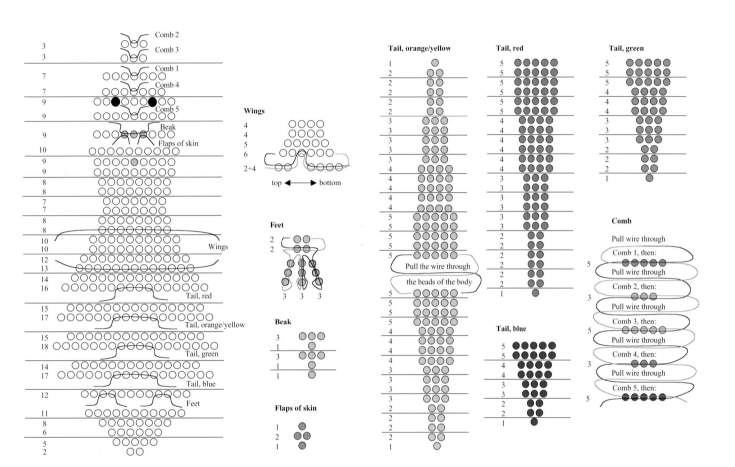

appendages are worked flat. Pay close attention to the deviating wire lead at the ends of the wings and feet. Craft the tail feathers three-dimensionally and attach them to the body by means of variant 1. **Note:** Start work on the orange/yellow tail feathers at the tip of the feathers. Only when you have com-pleted the orange section should you pull the two wire ends in opposite direc-tions through the appropriate beads on the body. Then you can craft the yellow tail feathers.

MATERIALS

- Rocaille beads in yellow, orange, bright red, dark blue, green, and white, size 8/0 (2.5 mm)

- 2 Rocaille beads in black, size 7/0 (3 mm)

- • Wire: 27 in (170 cm) for the body; 6 x 12 in (30 cm) for the feet, beak, wattles, and blue tail feathers; 4 x 16 in (40 cm) for the wings, comb, and green tail feathers; 20 in (50 cm) for the red tail feathers; 24 in (60 cm) for the orange and yellow tail feathers

13

Honey Bear

MATERIALS

- Rocaille beads in silver-lined brown (or mother-of-pearl chocolate brown), black, bright red, yellow, brown, and matte glass), size 8/0 (2.5 mm)

- 2 Rocaille beads in black, size 7/0 (3 mm)

- 1 Rocaille bead in black, size 6/0 (4 mm)

- Wire: 67 in (170 cm) for the body; 2 x 12 in (30 cm) for the ears; 2 x 16 in (40 cm) for the honey pot and bee; 4 x 28 in (70 cm) for the arms and legs

B rown bears are omnivores. This means that they eat not only meat, fish, and carrion, but also plants, roots, and berries. As everyone knows, though, bears' appetite for honey is the stuff of many stories. With the help of their firm claws, they can tear open bee-hives to get to the honey, and they're not bothered at all by the bees' trying to defend their hive, since their dense coats protect them from being stung.

Instructions

Use the larger beads for the eyes and the tip of the snout. As you craft the body, you will apply the seahorse technique for many sections. Attach the ears, arms, and legs to the body by means of variant 2. Apply the seahorse technique when you are shaping the crook of the arm. Do not cut protruding wire ends from the arm, since you can use them to attach the honey pot. Work the first four rows of each leg flat across the body before beginning to shape the legs three-dimensionally. Use the seahorse technique again when working with the feet. To prevent the legs from standing away from the body too much, you can secure them with a small piece of wire. When you work on the bee, start with the antennae; twist the wire to create a length of approximately 1/8 in (4 mm) for each. The brown rows of the bee remain flat. To properly shape the wings and to attach the bee to the honey pot, you will deviate from the basic threading technique (see illustration).

* Thread these rows in the order indicated by the numbers. For rows with two numbers, draw the wire through a second time to create two consecutive upper and two consecutive lower rows.

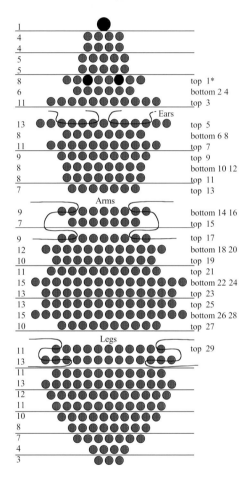

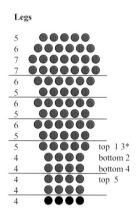

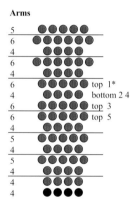

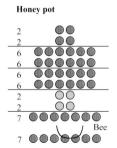

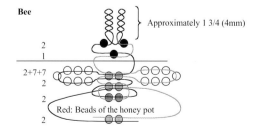

15

Wise Owl

In ancient Greece, the owl was the symbol of wisdom. While this perception of the owl as a wise creature has persisted into the present, the owl's impenetrable and stoic facial expression has also given it a bad reputation in the world of fairy tales. In some cultures, the owl is considered a sign of evil or death, and the bird's courtship calls are considered uncanny and perceived as a sign of bad luck.

Instructions

Use 6/0 (4 mm) beads for the eyes. To make the owl stand better, press the last three body rows slightly inward. Attach all appendages by means of variant 2. Work the wings, tail, feet, and bow tie flat, but craft the beak three-dimensionally. When you are crafting the bow tie, thread the first three rows; then pull one wire end through the corresponding bead of the body. Next, thread this wire end a second time through the third row of the bow tie. Then you can finish up the bow tie. For the mortarboard, I recommend

MATERIALS

- Rocaille beads in pale yellow, orange, reddish brown, and black, size 8/0 (2.5 mm)
- 2 Rocaille beads in black, size 6/0 (4 mm)
- Wire: 67 in (170 cm) for the body; 2 x 24 in (60 cm) for the wings; 7 x 12 in (30 cm) for the feet, tail, bow tie, beak, cord, and base of the mortarboard; 16 in (40 cm) for the top of the mortarboard

that you string the two rows of the cap base first. Lay the first row toward the back and the second row toward the front. **Note:** Do not cut off the wire ends of the cap base, since you can attach the cap lid with them. Craft the lid of the cap as an individual piece before

attaching it to the base. Likewise, attach the cord to the cap lid using variant 1. Shape the tassel of the cord from wire: tie several loops of one wire end together in the middle with the other wire end.

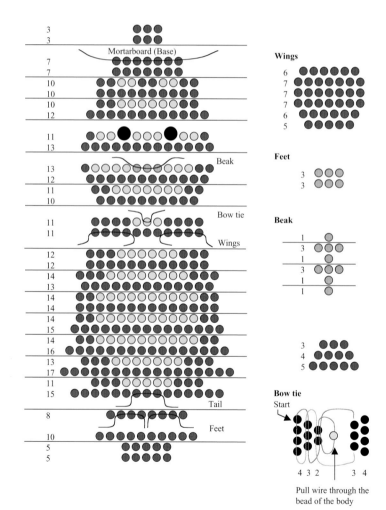

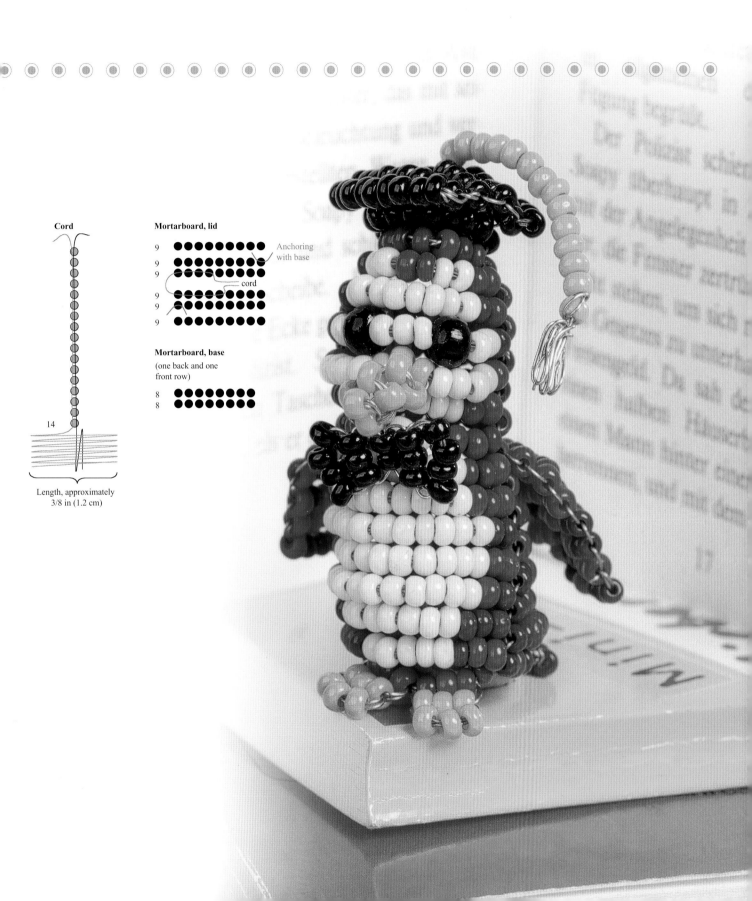

Cord

14

Length, approximately
3/8 in (1.2 cm)

Mortarboard, lid

9 ●●●●●●●●
9 ●●●●●●●●
9 ●●●●●●●●
9 ●●●●●●●●
9 ●●●●●●●●
9 ●●●●●●●●

Anchoring
with base

cord

Mortarboard, base
(one back and one
front row)

8 ●●●●●●●
8 ●●●●●●●

Weasel

With a body length of only 8 in (20 cm), the weasel is relatively small and lives in meadows and forests in rural areas. The weasel primarily hunts rodents like as rats and mice; however, it is known to eat bird eggs, birds, insects, fish, and amphibians as well. Its prey is often bigger than it is and is killed by a bite to the neck.

Weasels are very territorial and mark their boundaries with scent. Their young are born and bred in lairs.

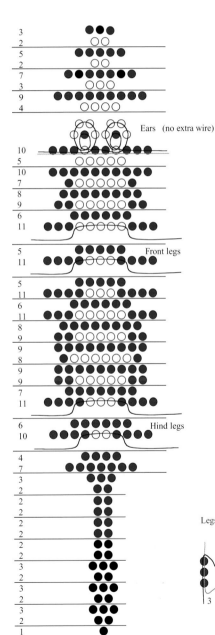

3	●●●
2	○○
5	●●●●●
2	○○
7	●●●●●●●
3	○○○
9	●●●●●●●●●
4	○○○○

Ears (no extra wire)

10	
5	○○○○○
10	●●●●●●●●●●
7	●○○○○○●
8	●●●●●●●●
9	●○○○○○○●
6	●●●●●●
11	●●●○○○○○●●

5	●●●●●	Front legs
11	●●●○○○●●●	

5	●●●●●
11	●●●○○○○●●
6	●●●●●●
11	●●●○○○○○●●
8	●●●●●●●●
9	●●○○○○○●●
9	●●○○○○○○●
8	●○○○○○○○●
9	●●○○○○○●●
9	●●○○○○○●●
7	●●●●●●●
11	●●●○○○○○●●

6	●●●●●●	Hind legs
10	●●●○○○●●●	

4	●●●●
7	●●●●●●●
3	●●●
2	●●
2	●●
2	●●
2	●●
2	●●
2	●●
3	●●●
2	●●
3	●●●
2	●●
3	●●●
2	●●
1	●

Legs

	2
	2
	2
	2
	2
3	

Instructions

Because our weasel figure is relatively small, a wire length of 60 in (150 cm) is sufficient. You should choose particularly large Rocaille beads for the black snout and the black eyes, so the face will show to advantage. In the fifth back row, make the ears using variant 5; no extra piece of wire is required. You can see the exact threading technique in the illustration. Craft the front legs and the hind legs three-dimensionally using variant 1. For each pair of legs, pull the 24-in (60 cm) wires through the corresponding beads of the eighth and ninth and the fifteenth and sixteenth belly rows, respectively. Note the special wire lead when forming the feet.

MATERIALS

- Rocaille beads in white, black, and brown, size 8/0 (2.5 mm)
- 3 Rocaille beads in black, size 7/0 (3 mm)
- Wire: 60 in (150 cm) for the body; 4 x 24 in (60 cm) for the legs

Fawn

D eer live in forests and land- scapes rich in undergrowth, where they form small herds that often consist of one family association. Young fawns hide in the grass when their mothers are not with them, but even when separated from her young, a mother can warn them of danger by firmly stamping her front hoofs on the ground and bleating an alarm call.

Fawns' white spots vanish with the first change of coat, at about three or four months of age; the males get their first, nonbranched, antlers at the age of four to five months. They shed their antlers annually, and new ones grow in their place.

Instructions

Use the seahorse technique for the fawn's neck, forming the shape first by a bend downward and then by a bend upward. Make the ears by drawing the 12-in (30 cm) pieces of wire through the corresponding beads of the seventh back row (variant 2). Create the front and hind legs three-dimensionally using variant 1. For one pair of legs, pull two 32-in (80 cm) wires each through the corresponding beads of the eleventh and thirteenth and the nineteenth and twenty-second belly rows, respectively. Note the special wire lead for forming the feet. To allow the fawn to stand better, weave the protruding wire ends into the visible wires along the sides of the legs and body.

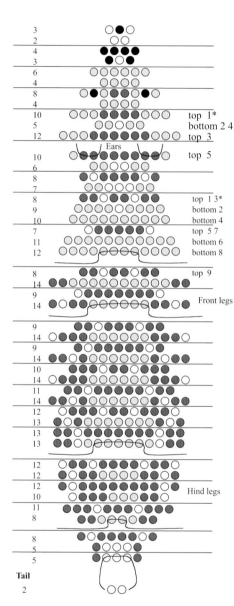

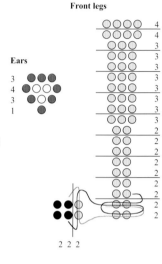

Front legs

Ears

Hind legs

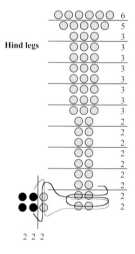

Tail

* Thread these rows in the order indicated by the numbers. For rows that have two numbers, draw the wire through a second time to create two consecutive upper and two consecutive lower rows, respectively.

MATERIALS

- Rocaille beads in white, black, reddish brown, and corn yellow or light brown, size 8/0 (2.5 mm)

- 2 Rocaille beads in black, size 7/0 (3 mm)

- Wire: 67 in (170 cm) for the body; 3 x 12 in (30 cm) for the ears and the tail; 4 x 32 in (80 cm) for the legs

Fox

⊙⊙⊙⊙⊙⊙⊙⊙⊙⊙⊙⊙⊙⊙⊙⊙⊙⊙⊙⊙⊙⊙⊙⊙⊙⊙⊙⊙⊙⊙⊙⊙⊙⊙⊙

The pointy-nosed head, the lean, stretched body, and the short legs are typical of the fox. These loners are predominantly active at dusk and at night and retreat into their holes to rest. Before any new litter, females expand their dens by adding extra tunnels.

Foxes catch birds by pretending to be dead, overwhelming their surprised prey. Behavior like this has earned the fox its reputation as a very cunning animal.

Instructions

Craft both the ears and the front and hind legs using variant 1. Draw the wires for the ears through the corresponding beads of the sixth and the seventh back rows; draw the wires for the legs through the beads of the tenth and eleventh and the sixteenth and eighteenth belly rows,

respectively. As you craft the legs three-dimensionally, pay special attention to the wire lead for the feet, which deviates from the basic technique. To better form the typical shape of the hind legs, thread the wire in the middle of each leg once more through the first bead of the previous outer row before stringing the next outer row.

MATERIALS

- Rocaille beads in white, black, reddish brown, and brown, size 8/0 (2.5 mm)
- 2 Rocaille beads in black, size 7/0 (3 mm)
- Wire: 67 in (170 cm) for the body; 2 x 12 in (30 cm) for the ears; 4 x 32 in (80 cm) for the legs

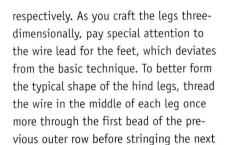

Front Leg   **Hind leg**

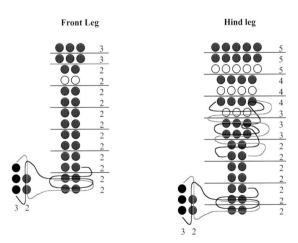

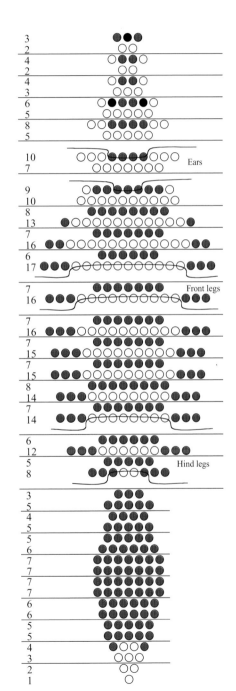

Ears

Front legs

Hind legs

Ears

Mole

Although the mole lives hidden in the earth, everyone knows it: the mole hills tell us where it lives. Underground, moles lay out a widespread network of tunnels with nesting chambers, ventilation systems, and passageways that run close to the earth's surface, where they search for earthworms, snails, and insect larvae.

Because the mole lives in the dark, its eyes are small and weakly developed. Its hearing, sense of smell, and sense of touch are, on the other hand, very sharp. Most striking about its appearance are the giant front paws that serve as shovels for digging.

These loners meet only in spring and early summer for mating.

Instructions

Form the front and hind legs using variant 2. When crafting the three-dimensional front legs, thread the 20-in (50 cm) pieces of wire through the corresponding beads of the eighth back row. As you form the paws, note the special wire lead. For the hind legs, draw the

two 32 in (80 cm) wires through the corresponding beads of the fourteenth back row. After you thread the following six rows, keeping them flat, pull the wire end, which points up toward the back, through the corresponding beads of the

nineteenth back row, from top to bottom. Next, thread the remaining beads of the three-dimensional foot. Bend the leg, which has been worked from front to back, forward at the spot marked by the arrow.

MATERIALS

- Rocaille beads in silver-gray or dark gray, pink , gold, and tan or light brown, size 8/0 (2.5 mm)
- Wire: 70 in (180 cm) for the body; 2 x 20 in (50 cm) for the front legs; 2 x 32 in (80 cm) for the hind legs

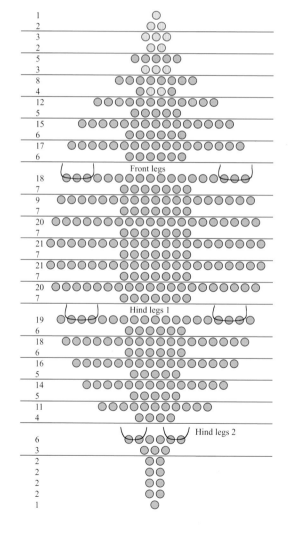

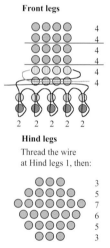

Front legs

		4
		4
		4
		4
		4
		4

2   2   2   2   2

Hind legs

Thread the wire at Hind legs 1, then:

	3
	5
	7
	6
	5
	3

Thread upper wire end (toward the back) from top to bottom through Hind legs 2, then:

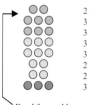

	2
	3
	3
	3
	3
	2
	2
	3

Bend forward here

25

Shrew

MATERIALS

- Rocaille beads in white, black, pink, brown, and light brown, size 8/0 (2.5 mm)

- 2 Rocaille beads in black, size 7/0 (3 mm)

- Wire: 51 in (130 cm) for the body; 4 x 20 in (50 cm) for the legs

Most shrew species live in forests and fields, hidden in the undergrowth and low groves. The house shrew likes to live close to human settlements. Despite their mouselike appearance, shrews are not related to mice.

Insects, spiders, and other arthropods are their primary food. Shrews have a rapid metabolism and are constantly in search of food. They are not at all social and live by themselves in fiercely defended territories.

Instructions

Note that the threading technique deviates from the basic technique after the second (white) bead: thread the third (brown) bead with one wire end before continuing with the normal threading technique from the fourth row on. Form the ears without any extra wire, as shown in the illustration (variant 5). Shape the front and hind legs three-dimensionally using variant 1. Pull the 20-in (50 cm) wires through the eighth and ninth and the twelfth and fourteenth belly rows, respectively. Pay close attention to the wire lead for the paws. Keep the tail flat. Use large black Rocaille beads to emphasize the eyes.

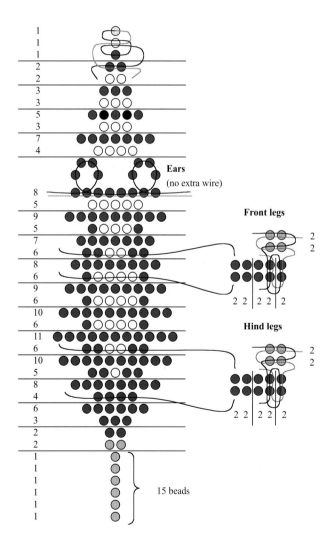

27

Lantern Bug

MATERIALS

- Rocaille beads in black, silver-gray or dark gray, blue, and yellow, red-striped translucent, and green-striped translucent, size 8/0 (2.5 mm)

- 2 Rocaille beads in black, size 7/0 (3 mm)

- Wire: 67 in (170 cm) for the body; 2 x 20 in (50 cm) for the wings

The lantern bug lives in the tropics and, despite its name, belongs to the cicada family. Each insect has its own territory: a tree trunk that is searched systematically at dusk and during the night from bottom to top for food.

The lantern bug's name is based on the striking extension from its head which, due to its bright coloration, suggests a lantern.

Instructions

Craft the legs with the body wire, as shown in the illustration (variant 5). Draw the wires for the wings through the corresponding beads of the eighth back row (variant 2). Work the left wing as a mirror image of the right wing. To prevent the wings from sagging, secure them with a small piece of wire at the back. Emphasize the eyes with shining black Rocaille beads.

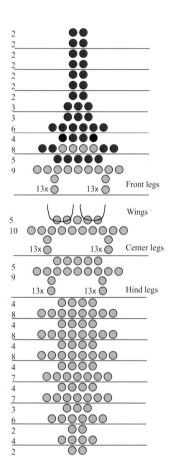

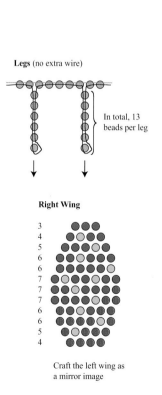

Legs (no extra wire)

In total, 13 beads per leg

Right Wing

Craft the left wing as a mirror image

Dog

Hunting peoples first introduced the dog into the household more than ten thousand years ago. It is possible that these hunters first tamed wolves, which then helped them while hunting. Since wolves are very social animals, working in a group would have been natural to them. Over the years, humans bred dogs selectively to emphasize certain preferred canine characteristics, resulting in more than a hundred different breeds recognized today.

Instructions

Note that the threading technique differs from the basic technique after the third row: pull both wire ends through the second row a second time. You will use the seahorse technique multiple times for the formation of the body. Use large (3 mm) Rocaille beads for the eyes and a 4 mm bead for the nose. Craft the ears and the tail using variant 2, keeping them flat, pulling 12-in (30 cm) wires

through the corresponding beads of the sixth and the last back row, respectively. Work the front and hind legs three-dimensionally using variant 1. For the legs, pull the 32-in (80 cm) wires through the corresponding beads of the ninth and tenth and the sixteenth and last belly rows, respectively. Pay close attention to the special wire lead when forming the feet.

* Thread these rows in the order indicated by the numbers. For rows that have two numbers, draw the wire through a second time to create two consecutive upper and two consecutive lower rows, respectively.

MATERIALS

- Rocaille beads in white and black, size 8/0 (2.5 mm)
- 2 Rocaille beads in black, size 7/0 (3 mm)
- Rocaille bead in black, size 6/0 (4 mm)
- Wire: 67 in (170 cm) for the body; 2 x 12 in (30 cm) for the ears; 12 in (30 cm) for the tail; 4 x 32 in (80 cm) for the legs

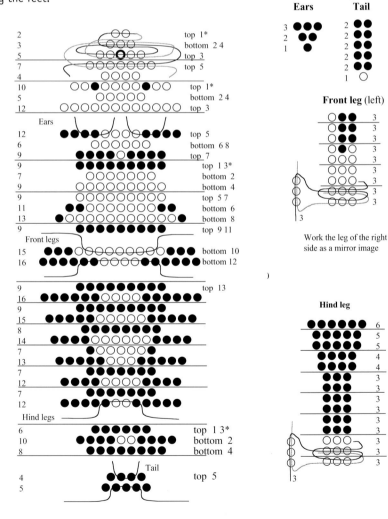

Work the leg of the right side as a mirror image

30

Young Seal

Young seals are sometimes called howlers because they howl if their mothers abandon them. This howling helps them stay in contact. These new-borns have a woolen white baby coat that later changes into a smooth, silvery light gray coat. The natural habitat of seals is the calm waters close to river mouths as well as tidal flats. Octopuses, coastal fish, and crabs are their usual food; for this reason, they were seen as competitors by fishermen and were hunted in earlier times.

Instructions

Thread the beads for the Young Seal onto the 67-in (170 cm) wire as shown in the illustration. Use a thick (4 mm) black Rocaille bead for the snout. Pay close attention to the special threading tech-nique used at the beginning. Work the front legs three-dimensionally using variant 1: thread one of the 24-in (60 cm) wire pieces each through the beads of the seventh and the ninth belly rows, as shown in the illustration. Work the hind legs three-dimensionally using variant 2; in this case, pull the two 12-in (30 cm) wires through the corresponding beads of the second-to-last belly row. Keep the ends of the feet flat.

MATERIALS

- Rocaille beads in black and white (silver-lined), size 8/0 (2.5 mm)
- 2 Rocaille beads in black, size 7/0 (3 mm)
- Rocaille bead in black, size 6/0 (4 mm)
- Wire: 67 in (170 cm) for the body; 2 x 24 in (60 cm) for the front legs; 2 x 12 in (30 cm) for the hind legs

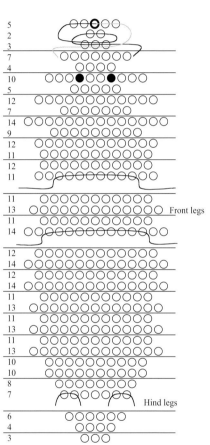

Front legs

Hind legs

Front legs

Hind legs

Red and Blue Poison Arrow Frogs

Frogs have special skin glands that secrete a substance that protects them against bacteria and fungi, for which the frog's sensitive skin would otherwise be an ideal environment. The secretions of the poison arrow frogs from the tropical rain forests of Central and South America are among the most poisonous biological substances known. The natives use these toxins to envenom the pointed ends of their arrows. The poison has a second function for the frog: it effectively protects it against predators. The frogs warn predators of this danger with their brightly contrasting colors; predators understand this as a signal for "Caution: I am poisonous!"

Instructions

Both poison arrow frogs are beaded in the same manner; only the colors of the beads vary. Craft the eyes, for which you should use the large black beads, with the body wire, as shown in the illustration (variant 5). Use a piece of 24-in (60 cm) wire for each of the four legs, which

are worked three-dimensionally (variant 2). Beginning with the sixth belly row, first work the front legs in the direction of the back of the body; then give them a bend forward in the middle; this is achieved through the deviating wire lead, as shown in the illustration. Start the hind legs from the last belly row, first directing them from the back to the front, and then bending them back at the spot marked by the arrow. Use the deviating threading technique shown in the illustration to create the flat feet, which point toward the front.

MATERIALS

- Rocaille beads in black and red or Rocaille beads in black, yellow, and blue, size 8/0 (2.5 mm)
- 2 Rocaille beads per frog in black, size 7/0 (3 mm)
- Wire: 60 in (150 cm) per frog; 4 x 24 in (60 cm) per frog for the legs

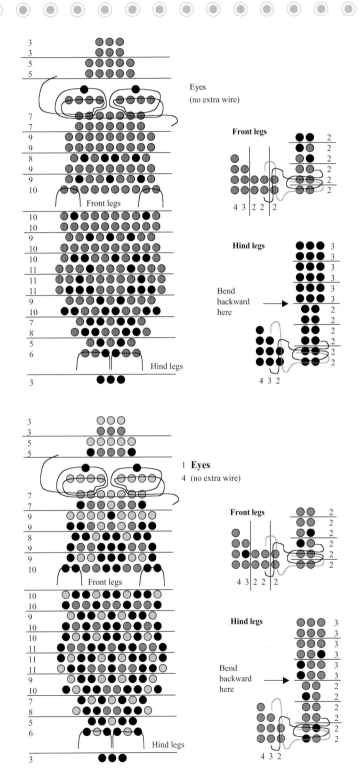

Common Green Darner

In the summertime, you can see the common green darner, which belongs to the dragonfly family, soar across ponds, lakes, and other watery places. However, the green darner can leave the water and even travel to the city. With some luck, you will find one around your own garden pond. Mature males patrol back and forth between different bodies of water and are constantly looking for female partners. After mating, females lay their eggs on plants near the water's edge. From the eggs come larvae that live for two to three years at the bottom of the pond before emerging and adopting their adult form.

Instructions

Work the eyes using variant 2. To thread the first row of the eyes, pull the wire through the beads of the back row, marked "Eyes 1." Next, pull both wire ends in opposite directions through the corresponding beads of the third back row; then, complete the eyes with the two following rows. Press the rows of the eyes flat onto the body. Apply variant 4 when working with the wings. It is important that the front wings hang over the back wings, as "Wing loop B" is used for both the front and back wings.

MATERIALS

- Rocaille beads in clear black, translucent, green, blue, and opal, size 8/0 (2.5 mm)
- Wire: 67 in (170 cm) for the body; 4 x 40 in (100 cm) for the wings

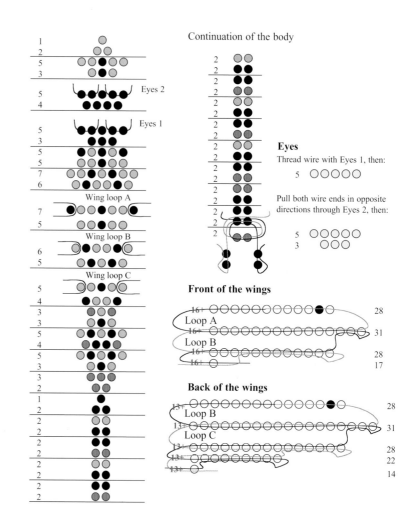

Continuation of the body

Eyes

Thread wire with Eyes 1, then:

5   OOOOO

Pull both wire ends in opposite directions through Eyes 2, then:

5   OOOOO
3   OOO

Front of the wings

Loop A   28
Loop B   31
  28
  17

Back of the wings

Loop B   28
Loop C   31
  28
  22
  14

Octopus

The word "octopus" means "eight feet"; the octopus catches its prey with its eight tentacles, with the help of its suction cups. Although it uses its tentacles to move, it can move even faster by a self-created jet propulsion of water. Also, when in danger, it, like the squid, can squirt ink, which acts as a screen to give it time to get away. The octopus can change its body color to blend in with its environment. At night, the octopus catches crayfish, mussels, and fish; during the day, it lies hidden among rocks on the ocean floor.

Instructions

When crafting the body, apply the seahorse technique, using a downward bend. Craft the eyes with the two 12-in (30 cm) wires, working from the upper side of the body toward the sides. Draw each of the wires laterally through the corresponding beads of two back rows.

MATERIALS

- Rocaille beads in white, light brown, and dark brown, size 8/0 (2.5 mm)
- 2 Rocaille beads in black, size 7/0 (3 mm)
- Wire: 67 in (170 cm) for the body; 2 x 12 in (30 cm) for the eyes; 8 x 47 in (120 cm) for the tentacles

Bend the row with the large, black eye bead upward between the first two eye rows. Attach the eight tentacles to the last two body rows (variant 2). Then apply the seahorse technique to create the tips of the tentacles.

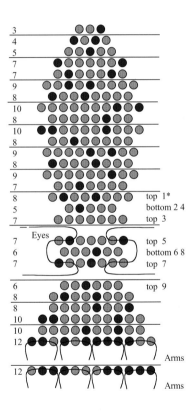

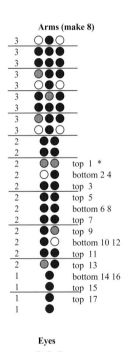

Arms (make 8)

Eyes

* Thread three rows; then thread the wire through the lower row once more to create two consecutive upper rows. The numbers indicate the order of the threading.

Orca

Orcas, also called killer whales, are the largest member of the dolphin family; adult males can grow to more than 30 feet (9 meters) long, and their dorsal fin can reach almost 7 feet (2 meters). Perhaps most striking about these mammals is the black and white coloration. Orcas live in all oceans; how-ever, they are particularly numerous in polar waters. They live and hunt in groups of thirty to fifty called pods, which is why they can overwhelm large prey, such as seals and other whales. Orcas use different vocalizations for echolocation and communication.

Instructions

Craft the pectoral fin and the caudal fin using variant 1. For the pectoral fin, pull two 20-in (50 cm) wires through the fifth and the seventh belly rows, respectively.

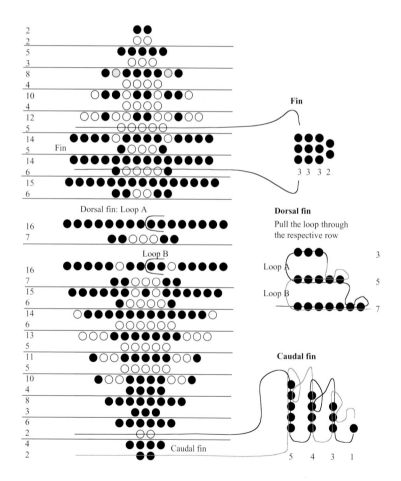

Thread two 20-in (50 cm) wires through the last two belly rows to create the caudal fins. Note the special wire lead.

Apply variant 4 to shape the dorsal fin, which requires a 16-in (50 cm) piece of wire. Note that here, also, the wire lead deviates from the standard.

MATERIALS

- Rocaille beads in white, black, and silver, size 8/0 (2.5 mm)
- Wire: 60 in (150 cm) for the body; 5 x 20 in (50 cm) for the fins

Clownfish

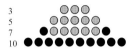

Clownfish get their name from their peculiar coloration. They are also called anemone fish, since they live among sea anemones. The anemones, or "flower animals," possess tentacles equipped with stinging cells that paralyze smaller animals, which the anemones eat. However, the clownfish are protected from the stinging cells by a thin layer of mucus on their skin. In this cohabitation or symbiosis, each of the two partners profits from the other: the fish are protected from predators by the stinging cells and the sea anemones eat the food remains of their tenants.

Instructions

Press the body slightly flat on the sides. For the flat, pectoral fins, pull the two 20-in (50 cm) wires through the beads of the sixth belly row as shown (variant 2). Work all other fins flat with the 16-in (40 cm) wires, using variant 3. Pull the wire of the first dorsal fin through under the seventh to the tenth back rows; pull the wire of the second dorsal fin through under the twelfth to the fourteenth back rows. For the anal fin, draw the wire through under the twelfth to the fifteenth belly rows. For the caudal fin, place a loop around the last belly and back rows. Note that the wire lead deviates from the standard.

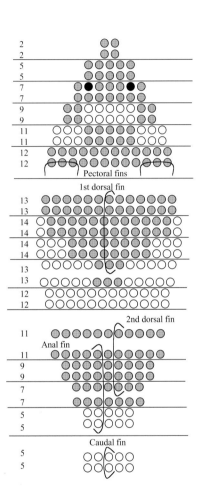

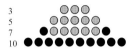

Pectoral fin

1st dorsal fin

Pull the wire through under the four back rows; then:

2nd dorsal fin

Pull the wire through under the three back rows; then:

Anal fin

Pull the wire through under the four belly rows; then:

Caudal fin

Pull the wire through under the last belly and back row; then:

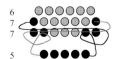

MATERIALS

- Rocaille beads in white, black, and orange, size 8/0 (2.5 mm)
- Wire: 67 in (170 cm) for the body; 2 x 20 in (50 cm) for the pectoral fins; 4 x 16 in (40 cm) for all other fins

Angelfish

Because of their sail-like fins, angelfish are among the most popular aquarium fish. Originally, they come from the area of the Amazon and Orinoco rivers and live in standing waters and calm streams. Often, they establish strong and lifelong partnerships that can last for up to fifteen years. Both parents guard their brood, which can number up to a thousand young ones, even sacrificing themselves to protect them.

Instructions

For the angelfish, thread the beads and press the body relatively flat on the sides.

No extra wire is needed to create the pectoral fins (variant 5). Work the dorsal and pectoral fins flat, using the 20 in (50 cm) wires (variant 4). For the dorsal fin, draw the loops through under the ninth to the twelfth back rows; for the pectoral fin, draw the loops through under the ninth to the twelfth belly rows. Pull the wire for the flat, caudal fin through under the last back and belly rows (variant 2).

MATERIALS

- Rocaille beads in pearl white, black, silver-lined transparent, and gold, size 8/0 (2.5 mm)
- Wire: 67 in (170 cm) for the body; 2 x 20 in (50 cm) for the dorsal and the pectoral fins; 16 in (40 cm) for the caudal fin

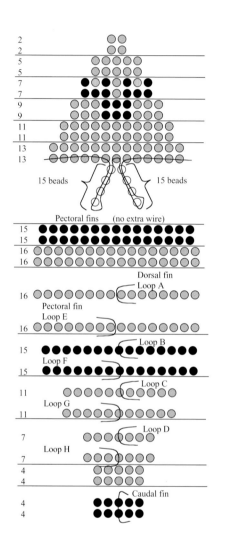

15 beads   15 beads

Pectoral fins   (no extra wire)

Dorsal fin
Loop A
Pectoral fin
Loop E
Loop B
Loop F
Loop C
Loop G
Loop D
Loop H
Caudal fin

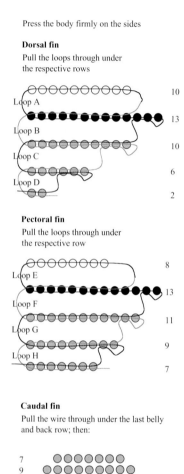

Press the body firmly on the sides

Dorsal fin
Pull the loops through under the respective rows

Loop A — 10
Loop B — 13
Loop C — 10
Loop D — 6
— 2

Pectoral fin
Pull the loops through under the respective row

Loop E — 8
Loop F — 13
Loop G — 11
Loop H — 9
— 7

Caudal fin
Pull the wire through under the last belly and back row; then:

7
9
11

Seahorse

The seahorse, named for its horse-shaped head, lives among sea grass in shallow waters, where it can anchor itself with the help of an extremely flexible prehensile tail. With its pipe snout, it catches small crayfish and fish larvae by ingesting the prey with a firm suction. The male possesses a sealable brood pouch located at the base of the abdomen into which the female deposits her eggs; the young ones can grow there protected from danger.

Instructions

As you form the body of the seahorse, apply the seahorse technique several times, using a downward bend. Craft the crown and the dorsal fin using variant 3. For the crown, draw the wire through under the fifth and sixth back rows; for the dorsal fin, pull the wire through under the twelfth and fourteenth back rows. Thread the wire for the pectoral fin through the corresponding bead of the fourteenth belly row (variant 2).

MATERIALS

- Rocaille beads in black, gold, and brown, size 8/0 (2.5 mm)
- Wire: 67 in (170 cm) for the body; 12 in (30 cm) for the crown; 16 in (40 cm) for the dorsal fin; 12 in (30 cm) for the pectoral fin

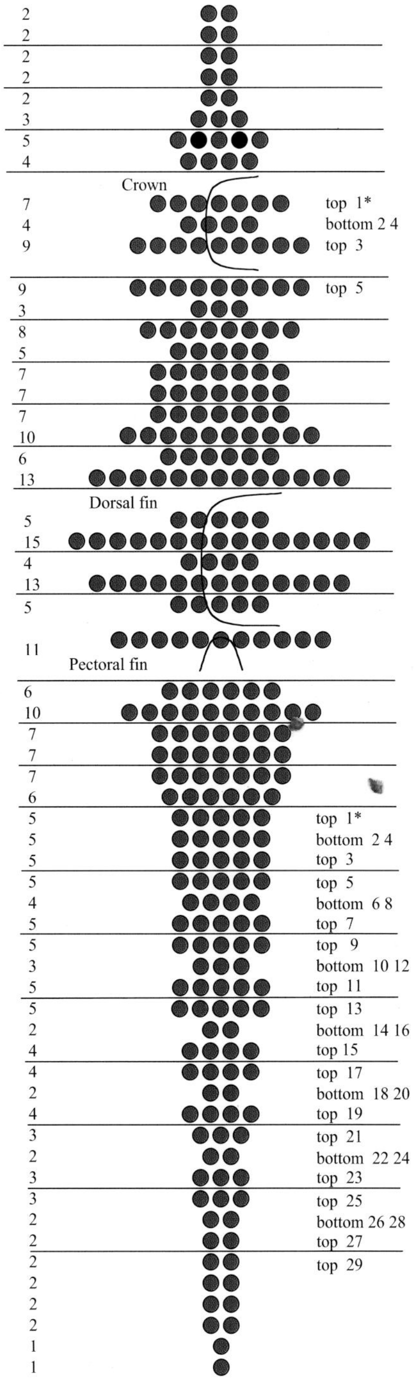

2
2
2
2
2
3
5
4
Crown
7 top 1*
4 bottom 2 4
9 top 3
9 top 5
3
8
5
7
7
7
10
6
13
Dorsal fin
5
15
4
13
5
11
Pectoral fin
6
10
7
7
7
6
5 top 1*
5 bottom 2 4
5 top 3
5 top 5
4 bottom 6 8
5 top 7
5 top 9
3 bottom 10 12
5 top 11
5 top 13
2 bottom 14 16
4 top 15
4 top 17
2 bottom 18 20
4 top 19
3 top 21
2 bottom 22 24
3 top 23
3 top 25
2 bottom 26 28
2 top 27
2 top 29
2
2
2
2
1
1

Pectoral fin

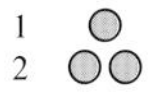

1
2

Crown

Draw the wire through under two back rows, then:

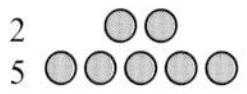

2
5

Dorsal fin

Draw the wire through under three back rows, then:

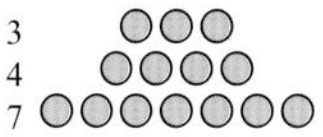

3
4
7

* Thread three rows; then thread the wire once more through the bottom row to create two consecutive upper rows. The numbers indicate the order of the threading.

King Penguin

King penguins populate Antarctic coasts and live in large colonies. The young are raised during the Antarctic summer, which extends from October to March. The female lays only a single egg, which she places on her feet and covers with a flap of belly skin to protect it from the cold. The parents feed their hatched young with small fish and crayfish only around every fourteen days. While they are young, king penguins are covered in simple brown downy feathers. Like all other penguins, these birds are unable to fly but live an extraordinary life on land and in the water.

ADULT PENGUIN

Instructions

For the neck, use the seahorse technique, with a downward bend. To allow the adult King Penguin to stand, press the last two body rows slightly inward. For the wings, thread a wire into each of

MATERIALS

- ⦿ Rocaille beads in black, black-striped translucent, blue coal, orange, yellow, and white, size 8/0 (2.5 mm)
- ⦿ Wire: 67 in (170 cm) for the body; 2 x 16 in (40 cm) for the wings; 2 x 12 in (30 cm) for the feet; 20 in (50 cm) for the tail

the body sides (variant 2). To represent the bend of the flat wings, the wire lead deviates from the standard, as shown in the illustration. Attach the feet to the body using variant 2. To form the tail, draw the wire through the fourth-to-last row. Lay the following two rows flat across the back; then pull both wire ends

in opposite directions through the indicated beads of the second-to-last back row, as shown in the illustration. Next, thread both wire ends in opposite directions through the second row of the tail before stringing the following rows of beads, keeping the tail flat.

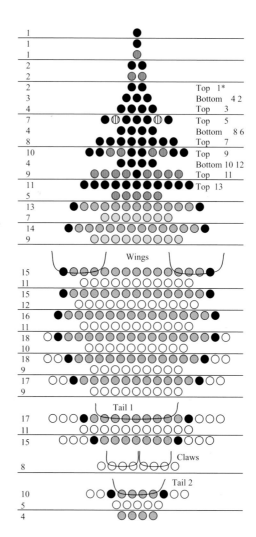

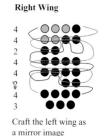

Right Wing

Craft the left wing as a mirror image

Claw

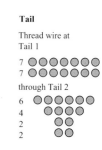

Tail

Thread wire at Tail 1

through Tail 2

* Thread the rows in the order indicated. For rows that have two numbers, thread the wire through a second time to create two consecutive upper rows.

BABY PENGUIN

MATERIALS

- ⊙ Rocaille beads in black, blue coal, and light brown (with a smoky silver coloration), size 8/0 (2.5 mm)
- ⊙ Wire: 43 in (110 cm) for the body; 2 x 12 in (30 cm) for the wings

Instructions

Press the last two body rows slightly inward so that the young bird is able to stand better. For each of the flat wings, thread a wire onto each of the body sides (variant 2). Form the feet and the tail with the wire of the body using the special wire lead (variant 5).

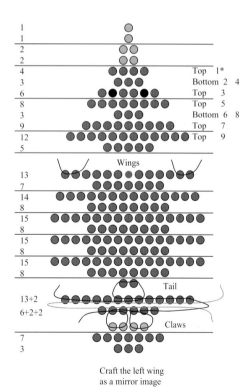

Craft the left wing
as a mirror image

* Thread the rows in the order indicated. For rows that have two numbers, thread the wire through a second time to create two consecutive upper rows.

The swan is rightfully renowned for its graceful S-shaped neck and orange beak. Swans eat primarily water plants and only rarely consume animals, but they are still known as omnivores. Swans nest on small islets in the reeds, where they build platform-shaped nests. In spring, the female lays five to nine eggs, which she tends alone. The male keeps watch and attacks any intruder—even a human—that dares to come close to the nest. Though their parents are white, young swans begin life covered with gray down.

Instructions

Apply the seahorse technique in two places on the neck, first with a bend downward, then with a bend upward. Use variant 2 to attach the wings to the body with a 51-in (130 cm) wire. Form the feathers on the edge of the wings as shown in the illustration. To prevent the wings from sagging, secure them with a small piece of wire. For the legs, draw 16-in (40 cm) pieces of wire through the beads indicated in the belly row, as

MATERIALS

- Rocaille beads in red, black, blue coal, and white, size 8/0 (2.5 mm)
- Wire: 79 in (200 cm) for the body; 2 x 51 (130 cm) for the wings; 2 x 16 in (40 cm) for the legs

shown in the illustration (variant 2). Pay close attention to the special wire lead on the feet. At the spot marked with the arrow, bend the legs forward. Keep the legs, wings, and tail feathers at the end of the body flat.

To stabilize the body of the swan and to better form the neck, work a wire in through the wires that are visible on the sides, as is done with embroidery.

* Thread the rows in the order indicated. For rows with two numbers, thread the wire through a second time to create two consecutive upper rows or two consecutive lower rows.

Wings (the right side points toward the back)

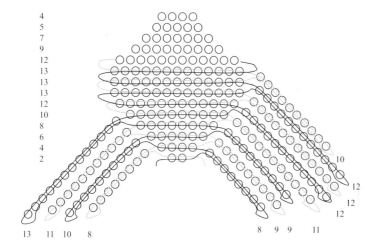

Leg

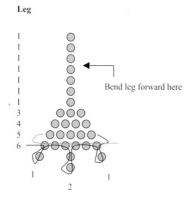

Bend leg forward here

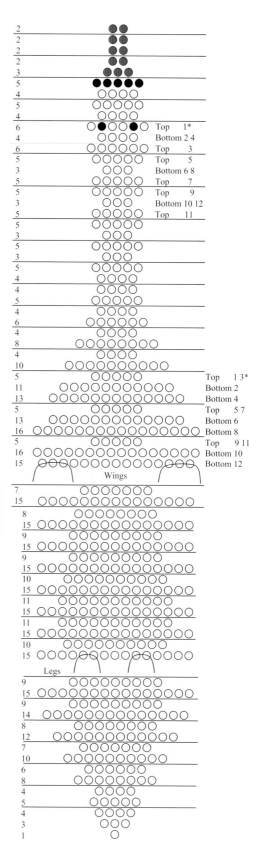

Marvelous Spatuletail

MATERIALS

- Rocaille beads in iridescent black, black, raspberry, orange, sky blue, pearl white, lime green, and jade, size 8/0 (2.5 mm)
- Wire: 55 in (140 cm) for the body; 4 x 24 in (60 cm) for the wings and tail feathers; 2 x 12 in (30 cm) for the legs

This species of bird, living in the high plateaus of northern Peru, is one of the 320 existing hummingbird species known today. Hummingbirds are very small birds which take in their food, such as nectar and insects, in a marvelous hovering flight. Also characteristic of these birds are the magnificently shimmering feathers. The male marvelous spatuletails have extended tail feathers that enable them to perform spectacular aerial stunts to impress females. Hummingbirds have a tendency toward polygamy, so one male may choose several females as partners.

Instructions

Keep the first three rows of the beak flat; bend the body rows open three-dimensionally. Draw the 24-in (60 cm) wires for the wings through the first and third lime green back rows (variant 1). Work the wings in a flat fashion; the tail feathers use their own wire lead, as shown in the illustration. Pull the short wires for the legs, which are worked according to variant 2, through the indicated beads of the fourth-to-last belly row. As you craft the tail feathers, note the special technique: start at the end of the lime green part. As soon as you have strung the eight lime green rows, pull one end of the wire through a border bead of the last body row. Next, twist both wire ends together for a length of approximately 2 in (5 cm) before threading the black iridescent part of the tail.

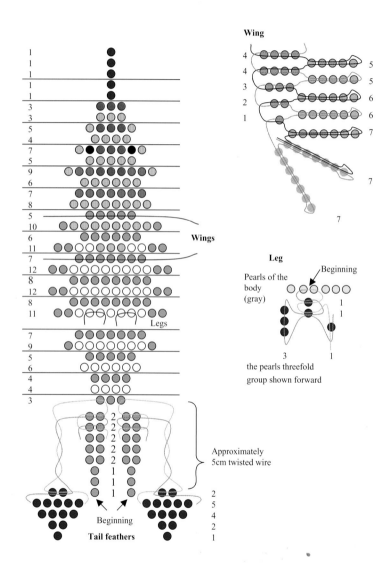

Wing

Wings

Leg

Pearls of the body (gray)

Beginning

the pearls threefold group shown forward

Approximately 5cm twisted wire

Beginning

Tail feathers

Legs

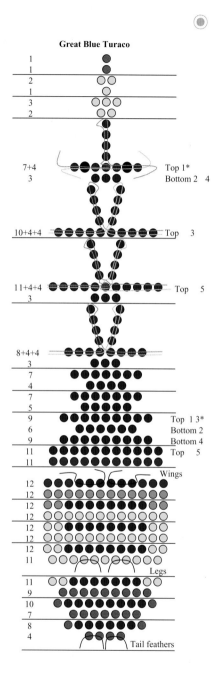

Great Blue Turaco

7+4
3

Top 1*
Bottom 2   4

10+4+4

Top   3

11+4+4
3

Top   5

8+4+4
3

Top   1 3*
Bottom 2
Bottom 4
Top   5

Wings

Legs

Tail feathers

* Thread the rows in the order indicated. For rows with two numbers, thread the wires through a second time to create two consecutive upper and two consecutive lower rows.

Great Blue Turaco

MATERIALS

- Rocaille beads in shimmering blue, black, red, yellow, light green, and dark green, size 8/0 (2.5 mm)
- 2 Rocaille beads in black, size 7/0 (3 mm)
- Wire: 70 in (180 cm) for the body; 2 x 20 in (50 cm) for the wings; 2 x 16 in (40 cm) for the tail feathers; 2 x 12 in (30 cm) for the legs

The great blue turaco is a relative of the cuckoo and lives in the rainforests of Africa. As the name suggests, the great blue turaco is anything but small, with a body length of approximately 30 in (75 cm). Because of its size, it is a poor flyer; it can, however, cleverly climb along branches. The bright blue feathers of the great blue turaco shimmer in the sun. Despite its vibrant color, the bird is almost invisible in the shade of the trees, as the feathers lose their brilliance when they are out of the sunlight. In this way, the great blue turaco is safe from its enemies.

Chipmunk

Instructions

Form the crown feathers on the head without any extra wire (variant 5). Use the seahorse technique for the neck. Keep the last ten rows of the body, which will become the tail feathers, flat. Use a separate wire lead for all other appendages (variant 2), such as wings, tail feathers, and legs, keeping them flat as well. Note the deviating wire lead for the legs. Stabilize the neck by working a wire in along the visible wires on the side.

MATERIALS

- ⊙ Rocaille beads in white (matte glass), corn yellow, black, light brown (sand), and dark brown (deer brown), size 8/0 (2.5 mm)
- ⊙ 2 Rocaille beads in black, size 7/0 (3 mm)
- ⊙ Wire: 20 in (180 cm) for the body; 4 - 20 in (50 cm) for the legs

Continuation of body
(continue to work from here in a flat manner)

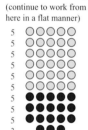

Legs

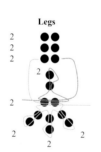

Left and right tail feathers

Wing

These cute animals live in North
America and are close relatives of
the local squirrels; however, they grow
only about half as big. Unlike the tree-
climbing, acrobatic squirrels, chipmunks
prefer to stay on the ground. They often
live in forests and eat nuts, seeds, mush-
rooms, fruit, and insects, which they col-
lect in their roomy cheek pockets. At
night and during hibernation, chipmunks
rest in underground burrows. Even during
rainfall, chipmunks remain in their burrows and then live on their carefully
hoarded supplies.

Instructions

For the eyes you should use slightly
larger black beads than you use for the
body. Form the ears in the sixth back row
using variant 5. At the base of the tail,
create the strong upward bend by
applying the seahorse technique once.
For the front legs, draw one wire each
through the eighth and ninth belly rows
and use variant 1. Craft the hind legs, on
the other hand, using variant 2: to
begin, thread the wire through the corresponding beads of the third-to-last back
row with a stripe pattern. Work the following four rows flat across the body.
Next, pull the wire end, which points
toward the back, from top to bottom
through a border bead of the last back
row with a stripe pattern. When you
work on the paws, which are worked flat,
note the special wire lead.

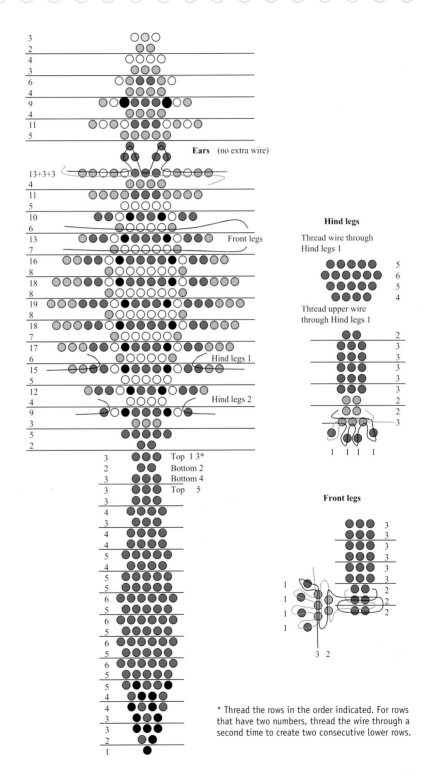

* Thread the rows in the order indicated. For rows
that have two numbers, thread the wire through a
second time to create two consecutive lower rows.

Great Anteater

A remarkable feature of the great anteater is its elongated head, ending in a very small, toothless snout. It has an extremely long tongue with which it can expertly catch ants and termites. Anteaters can be found only in South America, where they live in forests and on bushy savannahs. Great anteaters tend to move slowly and purposefully; they are solitary animals, their snouts always on the ground as they search for food. On their front paws, great anteaters have three long claws, which they use to tear open ant and termite nests. If threatened by a puma, a jaguar, or a human being, great anteaters can cause great injuries with these claws.

Instructions

Craft the ears of the anteater with a deviating wire lead (variant 5). Pull the four wires for the legs through the indicated beads of the eleventh and thirteenth and the seventeenth and second-to-last belly rows, respectively

(variant 1). Note when you shape the paws that the wire lead deviates from the standard. Pull the wire for the tail through half of the beads on each of the two last body rows so that the interfaces of the rows of beads are not on the sides but at the top and bottom. When you have finished beading, press the body flat slightly and the tail a bit more firmly.

MATERIALS

- Rocaille beads in white, black, beige, and brown (chocolate brown–mother-of-pearl), size 8/0 (2.5 mm)
- Wire: 63 in (160 cm) for the body; 4 x 70 in (50 cm) for the legs; 24 in (60 cm) for the tail

Hind legs

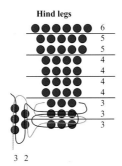

Front legs

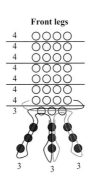

Tail

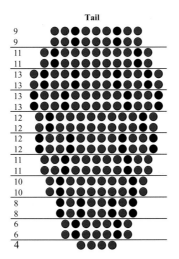

Great Anteater body

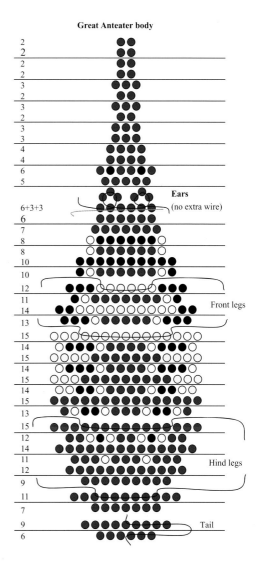

59

Emperor Tamarin

mperor tamarins are easy to rec-
ognize because of their long
moustaches. In fact, this particular
tamarin was given the name "emperor"
because of this impressive moustache.
This small monkey lives in the tropical
forests of South America and is quite
good at leaping from branch to branch.
Emperor tamarins live in small groups of
about ten animals that roam through the
forest searching for food. They eat small
animals as well as leaves and fruit. Each
group is led by a male and a female of
equal rank. The hierarchy of the group is
determined through threatening actions
and biting fights.

Instructions

As you craft the body, you will apply the
seahorse technique several times; first
create an upward bend, then a downward
bend farther on. Press the last two rows
of the body slightly inward so that the
monkey is able to sit. To shape the
moustache, draw both the leading wire
and several smaller pieces of wire
through the three beads of the snout.
Create a loop on each side of the lead
wire. Twist the moustache wires together
on both sides of the snout. Cut the individual moustache strands off at different
lengths: the length of the moustache
should amount to approximately 3/8 to

1/2 in (0.9 to 1.3 cm). Use variant 1 for
both the ears and the arms and legs. The
illustration shows through which rows
each of the wires is drawn. Shape the
legs using a deviating wire lead and work
them completely flat. To more firmly
connect them to the body, secure them
with a small wire. Attach the tail to the
body using variant 2.

MATERIALS

- Rocaille beads in brown, red-brown,
  red, black, white, and pearl pink,
  size 8/0 (2.5 mm)

- 2 Rocaille beads in black, size 7/0
  (3 mm)

- Wire: 60 in (150 cm) for the body;
  4 x 16 in (40 cm) for the legs;
  2 x 12 in (30 cm) for the ears;
  1 x 20 in (50 cm) for the tail

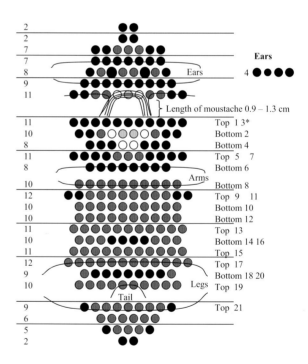

* Thread the rows in the order indicated. For rows
that have two numbers, thread the wire through a
second time to create two consecutive lower and two
consecutive upper rows.

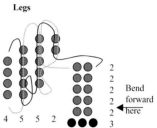

Legs

					2
					2
					2
					2 ← Bend forward here
4	5	5	2		3

Arms

2	
2	
2	
2	
2	
2	
2	
2	
2	
2	
3	

Tail

3	
4	
3	
4	
3	
3	
2	
3	} Repeat 8x
2	
2	
2	
1	

Kangaroo

The Australian kangaroo is the best-known member of the marsupial family. Female kangaroos have a pouch on their bellies in which the young, which are born extremely immature, are raised. The young one attaches itself to a nipplelike structure within the pouch and does not leave for a very long time. The kangaroo's strongly built tail plays a significant role in its familiar hopping motion. Kangaroos push themselves off with their tails and use them to keep their balance while jumping.

Instructions

For the eyes of the mother kangaroo, use slightly bigger black Rocaille beads than you use for the nose and claws. You will apply the seahorse technique several times as you form the body, using both an upward and a downward bend. Attach the flat ears to the body using variant 1, and the three-dimensionally shaped arms using variant 2. Create the bend of the arms from a deviating wire lead.

MATERIALS

- Rocaille beads in red-brown, corn yellow, and black, size 8/0 (2.5 mm)
- 3 Rocaille beads in black, size 7/0 (3 mm)
- Wire: 16 in (160 cm) for the ears; 2 x 24 in (60 cm) for the legs; 3 x 20 in (50 cm) for the arms and baby; 1 x 16 in (40 cm) for the pouch

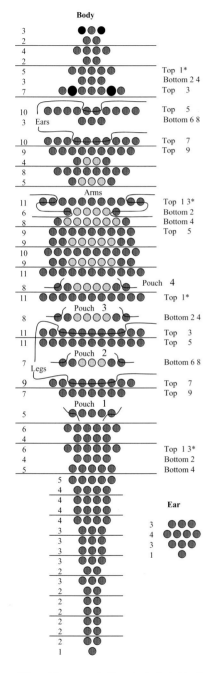

Body

3	
2	
4	
2	
5	Top 1*
3	Bottom 2 4
7	Top 3
10	Top 5
3	Bottom 6 8
Ears	
10	Top 7
9	Top 9
4	
8	
5	
Arms	
11	Top 1 3*
6	Bottom 2
8	Bottom 4
9	Top 5
9	
10	
9	
11	
8	Pouch 4
11	Top 1*
8	Pouch 3
11	Bottom 2 4
11	Top 3
	Top 5
Pouch 2	
7	Bottom 6 8
Legs	
9	Top 7
7	Top 9
Pouch 1	
5	
6	
4	
6	Top 1 3*
4	Bottom 2
5	Bottom 4
5	
4	
4	
4	
4	
3	
3	
3	
3	
2	
3	
2	
2	
2	
2	
2	
1	

Ear

3
4
3
1

* Thread these rows in the order indicated by the numbers. For rows that have two numbers, thread the wire through a second time to create two consecutive upper and two consecutive lower rows.

To craft the pouch, thread the initial four beads onto the wire. Next, pull each wire end on its respective side from inside to outside through the beads marked "Pouch 1" to set up to thread the second pouch row. Now pull each wire end on its side from outside to inside through the beads marked "Pouch 2," and to set up the third pouch row. Craft the two other pouch rows in this way as well.

Start the baby kangaroo by forming its snout first, using one of the large black beads. Form the baby's ears without any extra wire; instead, use a deviating wire lead. The beads of the pouch, marked "Baby," constitute the second-to-last row. Attach the baby to the pouch by threading both wire ends in opposite directions through these marked beads. Then thread the last row of the baby. Craft the legs of the kangaroo mother last (variant 1). Work the first five leg rows flat across the body. When you pull the upper wire through the second-to-last row toward the bottom, both wire ends should end up at the lower end of the body so that the lower legs can be crafted. Work these lower parts three-dimensionally. Again using a deviation of the wire lead, form the feet of the kangaroo in a flat manner. So the legs do not stand away from the body too much, secure them with a small wire to the body.

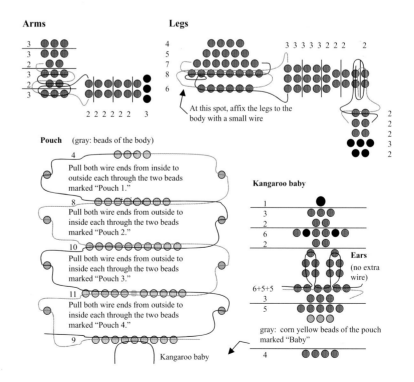

Arms

3
3
2
3
2
3

2 2 2 2 2 3

Legs

4
5
7
8
6

3 3 3 3 3 2 2 2 2

At this spot, affix the legs to the body with a small wire

2
2
2
3
2

Pouch (gray: beads of the body)

4
Pull both wire ends from inside to outside each through the two beads marked "Pouch 1."

8
Pull both wire ends from outside to inside each through the two beads marked "Pouch 2."

10
Pull both wire ends from outside to inside each through the two beads marked "Pouch 3."

11
Pull both wire ends from outside to inside each through the two beads marked "Pouch 4."

9

Kangaroo baby

Kangaroo baby

1
3
2
6
2

Ears (no extra wire)

6+5+5
3
5

gray: corn yellow beads of the pouch marked "Baby"

4

63

Horse

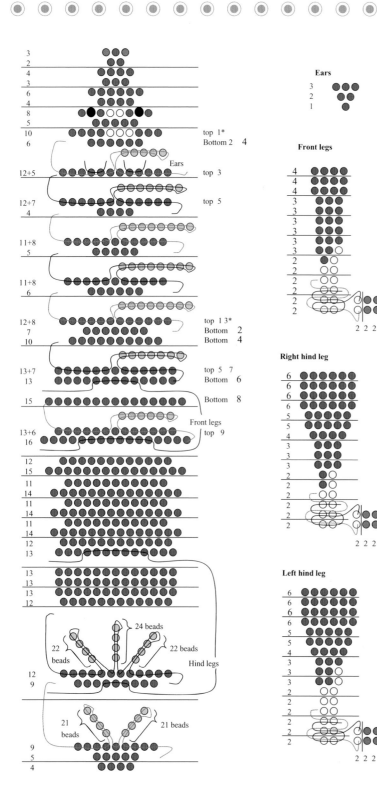

Ears

3
2
1

Front legs

4
4
4
3
3
3
3
3
2
2
2
2
2
2

2 2 2

Right hind leg

6
6
6
6
5
5
4
3
3
3
2
2
2
2
2
2

2 2 2

Left hind leg

6
6
6
6
5
5
4
3
3
3
2
2
2
2
2
2
2
2
2

2 2 2

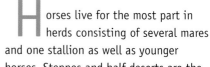

orses live for the most part in herds consisting of several mares and one stallion as well as younger horses. Steppes and half deserts are the usual habitat of horses. These environments provide little cover, though, so horses are always watchful and always ready for flight.

Originally, horses were widely spread across Asia, Europe, and Africa; today, however, there are hardly any horses living in the wild. For the most part they are kept as pets and work animals.

Instructions

As the wire required for the body is very long, I recommend that you use two wires, each 49 in (125 cm) long, and work the second wire into the figure as

MATERIALS

- Rocaille beads in brown, corn yellow or tan, white, black, gray (antique sterling silver or mother-of-pearl), size 8/0 (2.5 mm)

- 2 Rocaille beads in black, size 7/0 (3 mm)

- Wire: 98 in (250 cm) for the body; 2 x 12 in (30 cm) for the ears; 4 x 20 in (50 cm) for the legs

* Thread these rows in the order indicated by the numbers. For rows that have two numbers, thread the wire through a second time to create two consecutive upper and two consecutive lower rows.

required. For the eyes, use black Rocaille beads slightly bigger than the beads you use for the rest of the figure. Craft both the mane and the tail with the body wire, using a deviating wire lead. Apply the seahorse technique twice to the neck of the horse, first with a downward bend, then with an upward bend. Attach the flat ears to the body using variant 2. Use variant 1 for both the front and the hind legs. Form the hoofs via a special wire lead. The color of the horse shown here corresponds to that of a Black Forest horse, but you can easily craft your own white, roan, or pinto horse.

Guinea Pig

MATERIALS

- Rocaille beads in white, brown, and corn yellow or tan, size 8/0 (2.5 mm)
- 2 Rocaille beads in black, size 7/0 (3 mm)
- Wire: 63 in (160 cm) for the body; 4 x 12 in (30 cm) for the paws

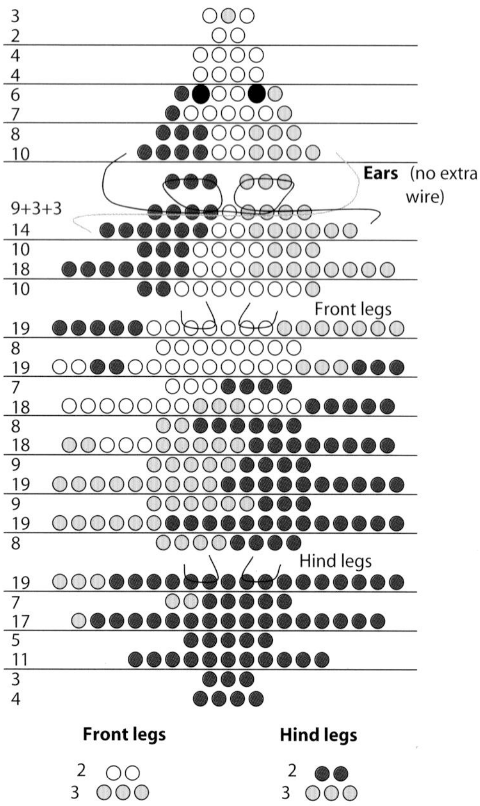
3
2
4
4
6
7
8
10
Ears (no extra wire)
9+3+3
14
10
18
10
Front legs
19
8
19
7
18
8
18
9
19
9
19
8
Hind legs
19
7
17
5
11
3
4
Front legs
2
3
Hind legs
2
3

Long before the Spaniards reached South America, guinea pigs had been domesticated by the natives, who allowed the animals to run freely inside and outside their huts. Guinea pigs were important for meat and sacrifices. The guinea pig makes a noise that sounds like the squeak of a piglet.

Wild guinea pigs, which have plain brown coats, dig their own burrows, an ability that domestic guinea pigs, which have variably colored and patterned coats, have lost.

Instructions

Crafting the guinea pig is relatively simple. As usual, for the eyes use black beads slightly larger than the beads you use for the rest of the figure. Craft the ears using the body wire (variant 5). For each of the four paws, pull a short piece of wire (variant 2) through the corresponding beads of the seventh and the thirteenth belly rows, respectively. If the rows of the belly gape too much around the hind legs, hold them together with an extra piece of wire. Press the last three rows of the body slightly inward so that the hind end does not come to a point.

Hare

ares tend to be solitary animals, which distinguishes them from the closely related but social wild rabbits. In addition, hares grow to be much larger and have longer ears than rabbits. Hares usually take flight when in danger, an effective defense, since a hare can run very fast for a very long time and can dart from side to side even at full speed. This abrupt change of direction causes many hunters to come up empty-handed. Hares are the only mammal that can survive even fierce winters without the protection of a cave or burrow. For protection hares press themselves into a flat hollow (sometimes called a form) on the ground, often under a bush or a log, and are very difficult to see.

Instructions

Use the large beads for the snout and eyes. Attach the ears and front legs to the body using variant 1. Although the ears are worked flat, you may bend the rows on the edge outward slightly to give the ears a more natural appearance. As you form the hind legs, thread a wire at Hind legs 1 first (see illustration). When you have completed the next five rows (worked flat across the body of the hare), pull the wire end that points toward the back from top to bottom through the beads at Hind legs 2. Then thread the other rows. Attach the tail to the body using variant 2.

MATERIALS

- Rocaille beads in brown and corn yellow or tan, size 8/0 (2.5 mm)
- 2 Rocaille beads in black, size 7/0 (3 mm)
- 1 Rocaille bead in light brown, size 6/0 (4 mm)
- Wire: 63 in (160 cm) for the body; 4 x 16 in (40 cm) for the front legs and ears; 2 x 20 in (50 cm) for the hind legs; 1 x 12 in (30 cm) for the tail

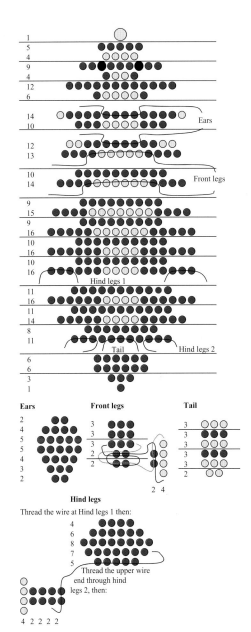

Violet Monarch Butterfly

Only a fortunate few ever encounter this species of butterfly. The males are widely known for the brilliant violet color on the upper sides of the wings; the females, on the other hand, are brown. The butterfly larvae feed on sorrel, which grows in dry, warm, and open areas.

Instructions

Form the antennae in the second body row using the body wire (variant 5). Twist the wire for a length of about ½ in (1.3 cm), after threading a black bead to the end to represent the knob of the antennae. For the legs, thread all nine rows; next, pull both wire ends through a belly row (but not in opposite directions). Then thread the beads for the opposite leg. Craft the wings using variant 4. When you work on the front wings, start with the upper edge. The front wings can be affixed to the body only after the second row; do this by using the loops shown in the illustration. The same holds for the hind wings:

start with the upper edge. When you attach the front and hind wings to the body, ensure that the front wings lie on top of the hind wings, using Loop B. Also, note the special wire lead on the edge of the wings. Work the left wings as a mirror image of the right wings.

MATERIALS

- Rocaille beads in white, black, gray (antique sterling silver–mother-of-pearl), shimmering blue-violet, and shimmering orange-violet, size 8/0 (2.5 mm)
- Wire: 47 in (120 cm) for the body; 4 x 20 in (50 cm) for the wings; 3 x 16 in (40 cm) for the legs

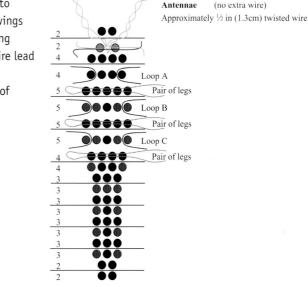

Antennae (no extra wire)
Approximately ½ in (1.3cm) twisted wire

Loop A
Pair of legs
Loop B
Pair of legs
Loop C
Pair of legs

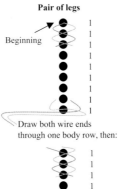

Pair of legs

Beginning

Draw both wire ends through one body row, then:

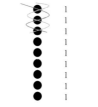

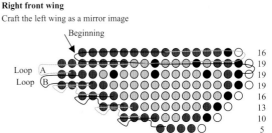

Right front wing
Craft the left wing as a mirror image

Beginning

Loop A
Loop B

16
19
19
19
16
13
10
5

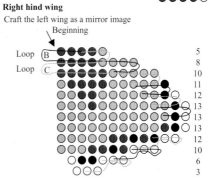

Right hind wing
Craft the left wing as a mirror image

Beginning

Loop B
Loop C

5
8
10
11
12
13
13
13
12
10
6
3

Alpine Newt

Although the alpine newt lives in lakes near forests, it also uses small ponds and even street gutters filled with water to spawn. When in the water, the newt stays mostly on the bottom. On land, it lives under rotten wood, in rodent burrows, or around tree roots, where it often hibernates as well. Between February and March, alpine newts wander to water to spawn; they leave at the end of August. During the spawning period, alpine newts are active both day and night. During the remainder of the year, they leave their hideouts only at night to look for beetles, flies, and earthworms.

Instructions

As the wire required for the body is very long, I recommend that you use two wires, each 55 in (140 cm) long, and work the second wire into the figure as required. Use the larger beads for the eyes. Craft the smooth crest and tail with a deviating threading technique, shown in the illustration. Form the legs using variant 1. For the front legs, pull a wire each through the eighth and ninth belly rows, and for the hind legs through the seventeenth and eighteenth belly rows. As you create the feet, note the special wire lead.

MATERIALS

- Rocaille beads in beige, black, orange, and water blue, size 8/0 (2.5 mm)
- 2 Rocaille beads in black, size 7/0 (3 mm)
- Wire: 110 in (280 cm) for the body; 4 x 20 in (50 cm) for the legs

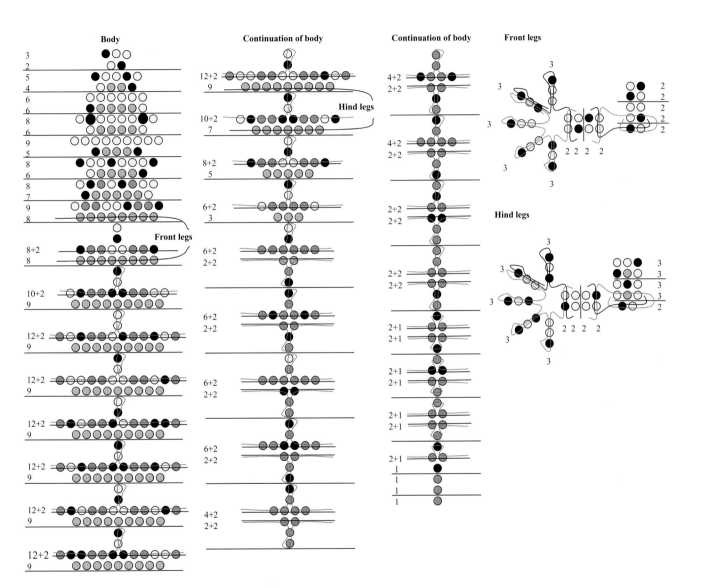

Body

3
2
5
4
6
6
8
6
9
5
8
6
8
7
9
8

8+2   Front legs
8

10+2
9

12+2
9

12+2
9

12+2
9

12+2
9

12+2
9

12+2
9

12+2
9

Continuation of body

12+2
9

        Hind legs

10+2
7

8+2
5

6+2
3

6+2
2+2

6+2
2+2

6+2
2+2

6+2
2+2

4+2
2+2

Continuation of body

4+2
2+2

4+2
2+2

2+2
2+2

2+2
2+2

2+2
2+2

2+1
2+1

2+1
2+1

2+1
2+1

2+1
1
1
1

Front legs

3
3
3
3
2 2 2 2
3

2
2
2
2
2

Hind legs

3
3
3
3
2 2 2 2
3

3
3
3
3
2

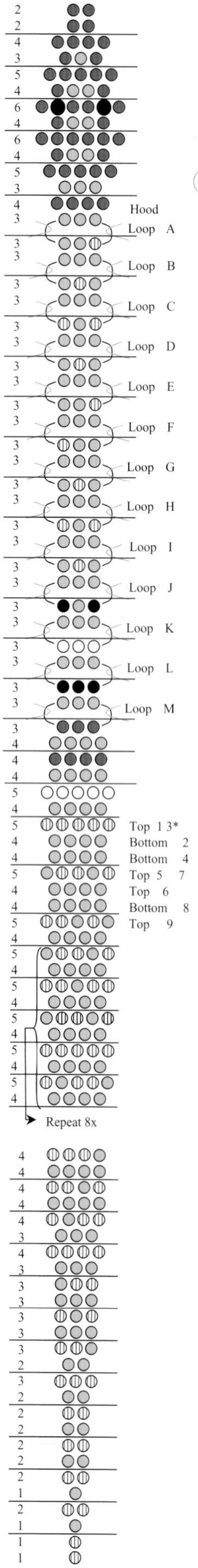
Hood
Loop A
Loop B
Loop C
Loop D
Loop E
Loop F
Loop G
Loop H
Loop I
Loop J
Loop K
Loop L
Loop M
Top 1 3*
Bottom 2
Bottom 4
Top 5 7
Top 6
Bottom 8
Top 9
Repeat 8x

Spectacled Cobra

Snake charmers use spectacled cobras, among others, for their shows. As the charmer plays the flute, the snake follows his movements with its eyes and body, thus creating the famous dance. Just as renowned is their characteristic hood: when frightened or expressing aggression, cobras expand their neck ribs to form a hood.

Hood (left part; work the right part as a mirror image)

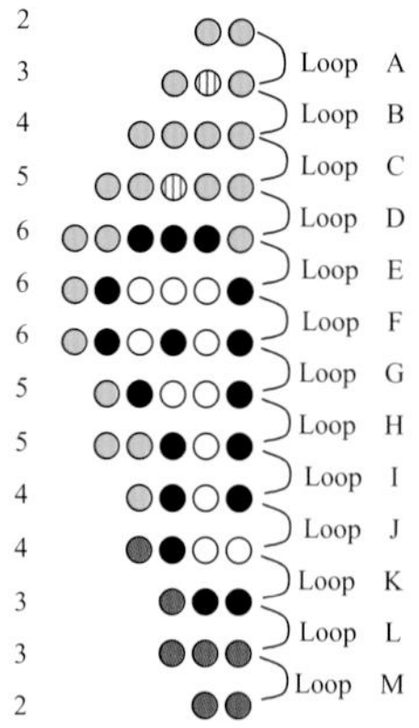
2
3
4
5
6
6
6
5
5
4
4
3
3
2
Loop A
Loop B
Loop C
Loop D
Loop E
Loop F
Loop G
Loop H
Loop I
Loop J
Loop K
Loop L
Loop M

Instructions

As the wire required for the body is very long, I recommend that you use two wires, each 63 in (160 cm) long, and work the second wire into the figure as required. With the exception of two rows for which you will create an upward bend using the seahorse technique, craft the body without deviating from the basic technique. Use variant 4 for shaping the hood; form each side with a separate piece of wire. To shape the lateral bend of the snake body, thread a wire into the wires that are visible on the sides of the body, as is done in embroidery. Position the head and hood vertically, leaning slightly backwards on the snake's body, and secure them there with a small wire.

MATERIALS

- Rocaille beads in light brown (apricot), brown, black, white, and red-brown striped, size 8/0 (2.5 mm)
- 2 Rocaille beads in black, size 7/0 (3 mm)
- Wire: 126 in (320 cm) for the body; 2 x 20 in (50 cm) for the hood

* Thread the rows in the order indicated by the numbers. For rows that have two numbers, thread the wire through a second time to create two consecutive lower rows.

PART TWO

Beaded Creature Jewelry

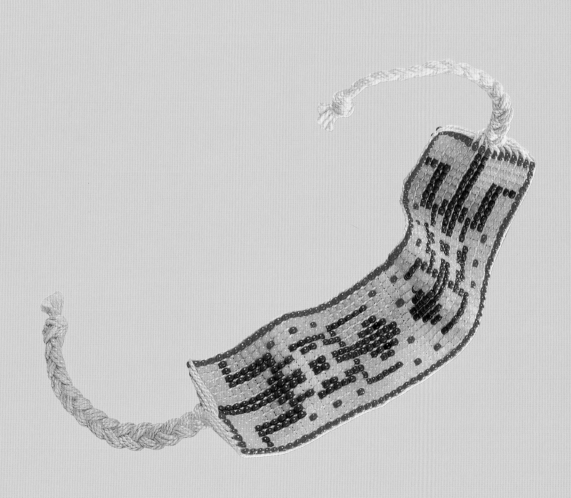

Getting Started

Materials

In addition to Rocaille beads, you will need the following materials to weave your beaded creature jewelry:

- ⊙ Bead-weaving looms, which you can purchase in various sizes at your local craft store
- ⊙ Mercerized or cotton yarn for stringing the warp threads; for the pieces in this section, a yarn weight of 5 was used
- ⊙ Transparent sewing thread or thin nylon thread (strength 0.15 mm or 0.25 mm) for stringing the beads (weft thread)

Tools

- ⊙ Thin sewing needle with a small eye or, if possible, a special beading needle
- ⊙ Scissors
- ⊙ Jewelry accessories, such as necklace clasps, brooch pins, barrettes, and key rings
- ⊙ Adhesive tape
- ⊙ A glue gun or other adhesive

Techniques

WEAVING WITH THE LOOM

Number and Length of Warp Threads

The length of the warp threads (threads in the lengthwise direction), made of mercerized yarn, should conform to the length of the finished weaving work; note, though, that this can sometimes mean that they should be approximately 16 inches (40 cm) longer than the finished weaving work, so that on both ends about 8 inches (20 cm) of thread remains for a final braid. The *minimal* length of the warp threads should be slightly greater than the length of the loom itself, so that you can stretch the threads on the frame. Also, when the weaving work calls for a pattern that is ten beads wide, you will need eleven warp threads, that is, one thread more than the number of beads in one row.

Warping the Loom

When you warp the loom, tie the individual warp threads to the upper end of the frame on the little warp beam. Then stretch the threads across the frame by stringing them tightly from top to bottom and from groove to groove; next, tie them around the wooden pegs on the lower end (web beam). To prevent the threads from slipping out of the grooves, I recommend that you secure the threads with a strip of adhesive tape just above the grooves.

Weaving with Beads

Tie the weft thread (the thread with which you weave), which is made from transparent sewing thread, to the left outer warp. Pass the weft thread from the left under the warp threads to the right side. Then, using a needle, thread the desired amount of colored beads.

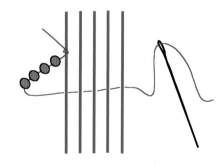

With your left hand, push the beads up between the warp threads so that a bead always alternates with a warp thread. Now, pass the needle from right to left back through all of the beads; as you do this, it is very important that you keep the needle above the warp threads.

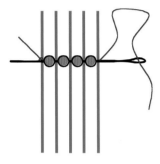

TIP: When you weave, do not start from the uppermost edge of the frame; rather, make sure that about 8 in (20 cm) of the warp threads remains empty from the small warp beam to the beginning of the weaving work.

Tighten the weft threads slightly after each row. Also take care that individual rows follow closely one after the other, and do not allow the rows to run diagonally across the warp threads.

Sewing Off the Weft Thread

When you sew off the weft thread, tie the thread on the left side on the outermost warp thread. After pulling the thread once more through a finished row of beads, cut it off.

Longer Weaving Works

There may be instances when your finished project will be longer than the loom. In this case, when you have filled the length of the loom with your weaving piece, you must loosen the warp threads on the lower end by untying them from the pegs and pulling them out of the grooves. Then wrap the woven piece around the removable crossbar on the upper edge of the loom. Next, attach the crossbar once more and stretch the warp threads anew so you can continue your project.

Decreasing the Number of Warp Threads

To create curves within the weaving pattern, reduce the number of warp threads. The procedure is as follows:

1. In the row with the maximum number of beads, tie the weft thread to the outermost warp thread on the side on which the number of warp threads is supposed to be reduced.

2. Tie the weft thread around the two outermost warp threads and secure them with another knot. (If the number of warp threads is supposed to be reduced by more than one, simply entwine that many warp threads with the weft thread and tie them together.)

3. Before threading the second shortened row of beads, tie the two lateral warp threads once again.

4. Before threading the third shortened row of beads, once again tie the two lateral warp threads.

5. The warp thread that is no longer necessary can be cut off (provided that the number of beads per row is not increased once again later on), and the piece can be continued in the usual way.

Finishing

To finish a piece of work (for instance, a wristband), simply braid the warp threads and knot the ends.

Reduction to the left   Reduction to the right

(1)
(2)   (1)
(3)   (2)
(4)   (3)
(5)   (4)
                                   (5)

Other beads can still be worked into the braid for ornamentation. With the necklaces, for example, a clasp is attached to the concluding braid.

African Animal Motif

○ ● ○ ● ○ ● ○ ● ○ ● ○ ● ○ ● ○ ● ○ ● ○ ● ○ ● ○ ● ○ ● ○ ● ○ ● ○ ● ○ ● ○ ● ○

Perhaps the most striking characteristic about African art is the highly stylized presentation of the animals. These animals can serve as the basis for dazzling geometric ornaments. This particular stylized motif has its origin in Ghana in West Africa.

Fringe made from 14 beads alternating with braid

KEY-RING PENDANT

Instructions

Stretch the 17 yellow 8-in (20 cm) warp threads onto the weaving loom. (If the loom happens to be longer, the warp threads must be at least as long as the loom.)

MATERIALS

- ⦿ Rocaille beads in yellow, orange, black, red, and brown, size 8/0 (2.5 mm)
- ⦿ 17 warp threads made from mercerized yarn (5), 8 in (20 cm) long, in yellow
- ⦿ Weaving loom
- ⦿ Beading needle
- ⦿ Transparent sewing thread
- ⦿ Key ring

Next, weave the beads according to the sample illustration.

To finish, make two short braids at the upper end; then knot them together through the loop of the key ring. At the lower end, make three small braids and knot the ends. For the beaded fringes, tie a new piece of transparent sewing thread on the lower outer edge and thread 13 red Rocaille beads and one orange one.

Pull the thread back through the just-strung beads (with the exception of the lowest, orange, one). Next, pull the thread through the beads of the bottom row of the weaving work and in between the subsequent two braids. Here, again string 14 Rocaille beads, and pull the thread back once more through the threaded beads, and so on.

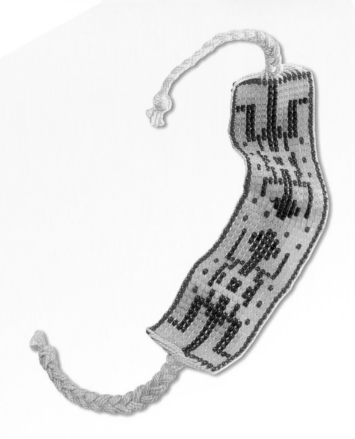

WRISTBAND

Instructions

Stretch 17 warp threads on the weaving loom. Use yellow mercerized yarn for the 24-in (60 cm) warp threads. Weave the wristband, using the illustration as your guide. A braid on each side, with a knot at the end, serves as a concluding ornament.

MATERIALS

- Rocaille beads in yellow, orange, black, red, and brown, size 8/0 (2.5 mm)
- 17 warp threads made from mercerized yarn (5), 24 in (60 cm) long, in yellow
- Weaving loom
- Beading needle
- Transparent sewing thread

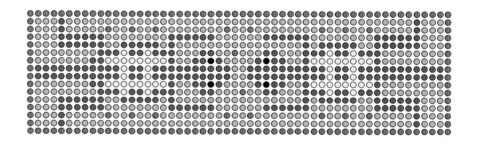

Wristband with Bird Motif

MATERIALS

- Rocaille beads in ultramarine, pastel orchid, pastel lilac, pastel pink, green, May green, pastel green, orange, yellow, and pastel yellow, size 8/0 (2.5 mm)
- 16 warp threads made from mercerized yarn (5 g), 24 in (60 cm) long, with blue-lilac streak
- Weaving loom
- Beading needle
- Transparent sewing thread

You will find the original of this bird motif on a cloak from Guatemala. Most characteristic of this pattern are the bright colors.

Instructions

Stretch 16 warp threads on the weaving loom. Weave the wristband, using the illustration as a guide. To finish, make a braid on each side, with a knot at the end.

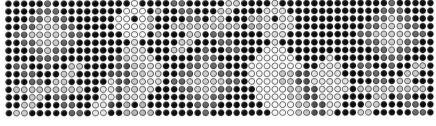

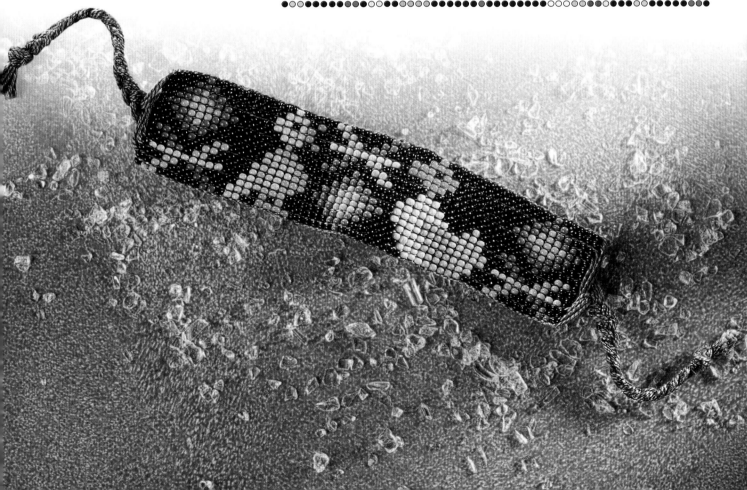

Peruvian Snakes

This snake motif originates from Peru. Several strongly stylized snakes wind across the ornament and endow it with a certain liveliness.

WRISTBAND

Instructions

Stretch 14 green warp threads on the weaving loom. The warp threads should be approximately 24 in (60 cm) long. Weave the wristband, using the illustration as your guide. Next, divide the warp threads into three strands on each side. String three 5-mm Rocaille beads of different colors onto each of these strands before making a finishing braid, ending with a knot.

BARRETTE

A barrette in the same pattern would perfectly complement this striking wristband. If you like, work the pattern as described here, but with a narrower width.

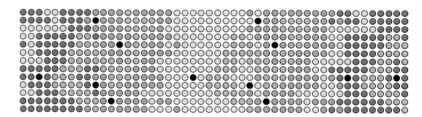

MATERIALS

- Rocaille beads in yellow, orange, black, green, fir green, and fir green (matte glass), size 8/0 (2.5 mm)
- Rocaille beads in green, yellow, orange, and black, size 5/0 (5 mm)
- 14 warp threads made from mercerized yarn (5), 24 in (60 cm) long, in green
- Weaving loom
- Beading needle
- Transparent sewing thread

Bird Brooch

The colors in the bird brooch coordinate well with those of the Wristband with Bird Motif.

Instructions

Work the first three rows of the beak flat. Bend all other body rows open three-dimensionally, but leave the last six rows for the tail feathers flat. Draw the 24-in (60 cm) wires for the wings through the indicated back rows (variant 1). Work the wings flat; note that the feathers point backward. When crafting the wings, pay close attention to the

deviating wire lead (see illustration). Attach the brooch pin to the belly of the bird with a short wire. First, draw the wire through the beads marked "Brooch pin 1"; then pull both wire ends through the two holes of the pin and then through the beads marked "Brooch pin 2." Instead of the brooch pin, you may want to give the bird legs: pull the short

wires for the legs (which are worked according to variant 2) through the indicated beads of the fourth-to-last belly row.

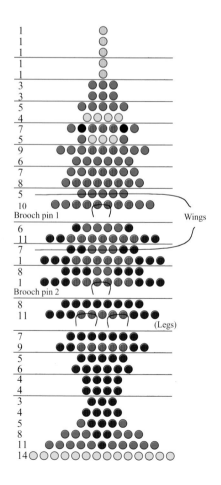

MATERIALS

- Rocaille beads in black, orange, ultramarine, yellow, May green, and pastel orchid, size 8/0 (2.5 mm)
- Wire: 60 in (150 cm) for the body; 2 ? 24 in (60 cm) for the wings; 1 ? 12 in (30 cm) for the attachment of the brooch pin (or 2 x 12 in (30 cm) for the legs)
- 1 brooch pin, ¾ in (19 mm), with safety catch

Wings

The feathers point toward the back

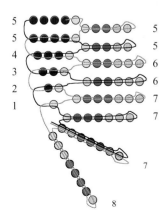

5
5
4
3
2
1

5
5
5
6
6
7
7

7

8

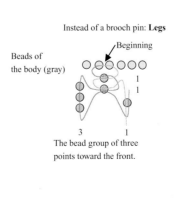

Instead of a brooch pin: **Legs**

Beginning

Beads of
the body (gray)

1
1

3   1

The bead group of three
points toward the front.

Lizard Motifs

Lizards and reptiles are popular motifs in many cultures. Particularly well known are the Australian and stylized African representations.

WRISTBAND

Instructions

Stretch 15 white warp threads on the weaving loom. Weave the wristband, using the illustration as a guide. To finish, make a braid on each side, ending with a knot.

MATERIALS

- 15 warp threads made from mercerized yarn (5), 24 in (60 cm) long, in white
- Weaving loom
- Beading needle
- Rocaille beads in corn yellow (matte glass), white (matte glass), white, black, eggplant, red, and brown, size 8/0 (2.5 mm)
- Transparent sewing thread

NECKLACE

Instructions

Stretch 15 white warp threads of 30 in (75 cm) on the weaving loom. Weave the wristband, using the illustration as a guide. **Note:** Start weaving approximately 10 in (25 cm) from the warp beam, beginning with one of the first rows with a complete number of beads (see illustration). Then finish the band, working in both directions. The number of warp threads on both sides is decreased step by step to five (see "Decreasing the Number of Warp Threads" under "Techniques," earlier).

The length of the necklace can be made to suit your individual taste by adjusting the length of the concluding braids. Attach the clasp at the end of the braids.

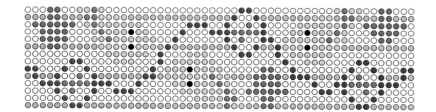

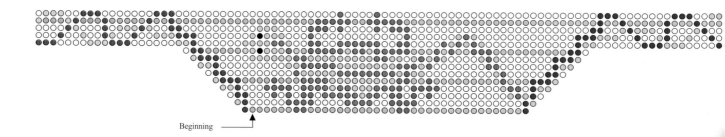

Beginning

MATERIALS

- Rocaille beads in corn yellow (matte glass), white (matte glass), white, black, eggplant, red, and brown, size 8/0 (2.5 mm)
- 15 warp threads made from mercerized yarn (5), 30 in (75 cm), in white
- Weaving loom
- Beading needle
- Transparent sewing thread
- Silver clasp

BROOCH

The design of this animal suggests one of those wall lizards that are frequently found in the Mediterranean area. As its name suggests, this animal likes to rest and sunbathe on stones and walls.

Instructions

Craft the body according to the technique explained under "Basic Technique" in the "Techniques" section of part 1. For the front legs, pull a wire each through the eighth and ninth rows, respectively, and, for the hind legs, through the seventeenth and eighteenth belly rows (variant 1). When crafting the feet, pay attention to the special wire lead; keep the toes flat. To give the tail and body a slight bend to the right and left, pull the protruding wire ends (or a new wire) tightly through between the visible wires on the sides, as is done in embroidery. Attach the brooch pin with a short wire on the lizard's belly. First, draw the wire through the beads marked "Brooch pin 1"; next, pull both wire ends through the two holes of the pin, and then through the beads marked "Brooch pin 2."

MATERIALS

- Rocaille beads in corn yellow (matte glass), white (matte glass), black, and brown, size 8/0 (2.5 mm)

- Wire: 70 in (180 cm) for the body; 4 x 20 in (50 cm) for the legs; 1 x 12 in (30 cm) for the attachment of the brooch pin

- 1 brooch pin, ¾ in (19 mm), with safety catch

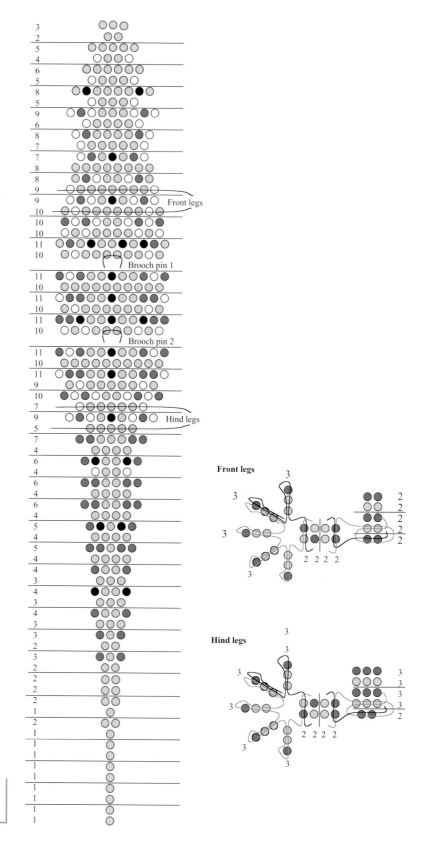

Butterfly Jewelry

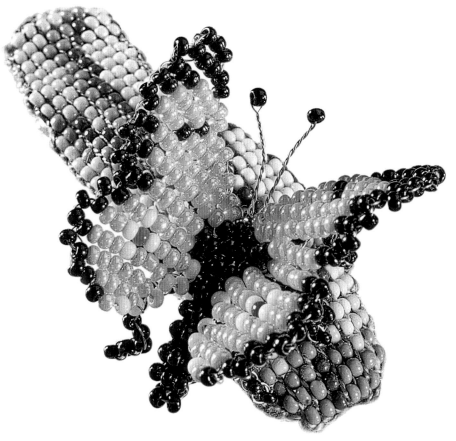

The blue-violet wings of the purple emperor butterfly shimmer in the sun, and it prefers to sojourn in deciduous forests close to creeks and ponds or along moist paths. The clouded yellow butterfly is a typical migrating butterfly. In warm years, it can wander from southern Europe all the way to Germany, though it often does not survive the harsh winters.

BROOCH AND BARRETTE

Instructions

The body is crafted in the same manner for both butterflies. Form the antennae in the second body row using the body wire. Thread a black bead, representing the knob of the antennae, onto the wire, and twist the wire for a length of approximately ½ in (1.3 cm). For each pair of legs, you will need a short piece of wire. String the nine rows of one leg first, and then pull both wire ends through a belly row (but not in opposite directions); then thread the beads for the opposite leg. Attach the wings to the body using variant 4. With the front wings, it is best to start with the lower edge of the wing; with the hind wing start with the upper edge of the wing. Be sure that the front wings come to rest above the hind wings with Loop B. Also, pay close attention to the special

MATERIALS
for Purple Emperor
Butterfly Brooch

- Rocaille beads in white, metallic lilac, black, silver-gray (silver lining), and orange (opaque, shiny), size 8/0 (2.5 mm)

- Wire: 12 in (120 cm) for the body; 4 x 24 in (60 cm) for the wings; 3 x 16 in (40 cm) for the legs; 1 x 12 in (30 cm) for the attachment of the brooch pin

- 1 brooch pin, ¾ in (19 mm), with safety catch

MATERIALS
for Clouded Yellow
Butterfly on Leaf Barrette

- Rocaille beads in black, silver-gray (silver lining), orange (opaque, shiny), bright red, pale orange, pale green, May green, green, and fir green, size 8/0 (2.5 mm)

- Wire: 47 in (120 cm) for the body; 4 x 24 in (60 cm) for the wings; 3 x 16 in (40 cm) for the legs

wire lead on the edges of the wings. The left wings are crafted as mirror images of the right ones. To attach the brooch pin to the body of the purple emperor butterfly, first, draw

rough the beads marked "Brooch pin 1"; next, pull both wire ends through the two holes of the pin, and then through the beads marked "Brooch pin 2." The clouded yellow butterfly is attached to a leaf barrette.

Body and legs for both butterflies

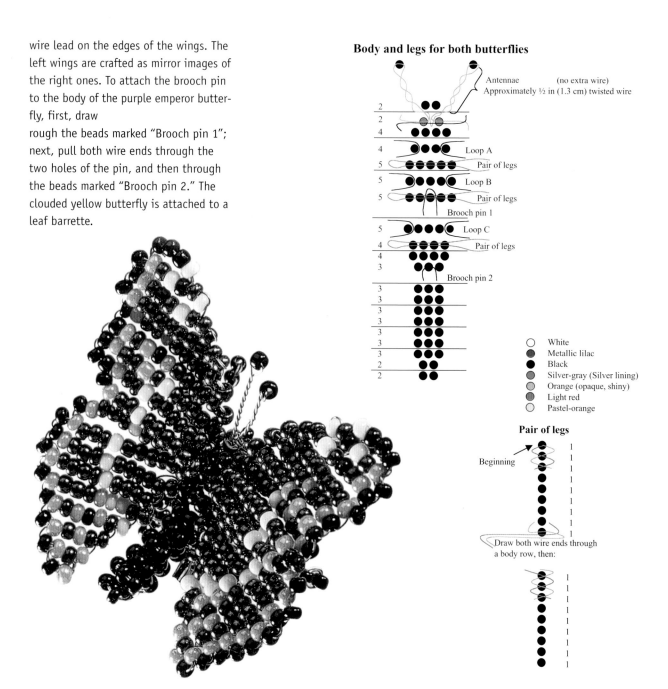

Antennae   (no extra wire)
Approximately ½ in (1.3 cm) twisted wire

2
2
4
4   Loop A
5   Pair of legs
5   Loop B
5   Pair of legs
Brooch pin 1
5   Loop C
4   Pair of legs
4
3
Brooch pin 2
3
3
3
3
3
3
2
2

○ White
● Metallic lilac
● Black
● Silver-gray (Silver lining)
○ Orange (opaque, shiny)
● Light red
○ Pastel-orange

Pair of legs

Beginning

1
1
1
1
1
1
1

Draw both wire ends through a body row, then:

1
1
1
1
1
1
1

Wings of the Purple Emperor

Right front wing

Craft the left wing as a mirror image

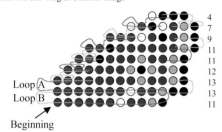

4
7
9
11
11
12
13
13
11

Loop A
Loop B

Beginning

Right hind wing

Craft the left wing as a mirror image

Beginning

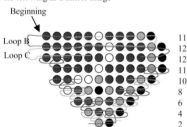

Loop B
Loop C

11
12
12
11
10
8
6
4
2

Wings of the Clouded Yellow

Right front wing

Craft the left wing as a mirror image

3
6
8
10
11
11
11
10

Loop A
Loop B

Beginning

Right hind wing

Craft the left wing as a mirror image

Beginning

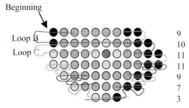

Loop B
Loop C

9
10
11
11
9
7
3

Leaf for Barrette

Do not cut off the wrap threads in this area

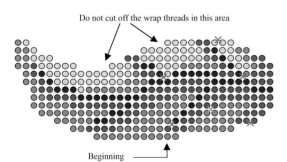

Beginning

91

Index